ABANDONED MONTGOMERY

RUINS OF THE CONFEDERATE CAPITOL

DAVID BULIT

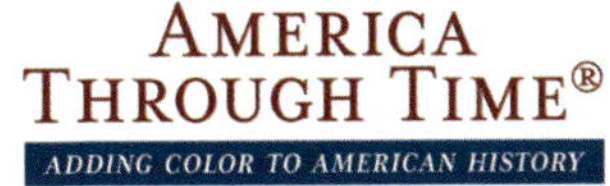

This book is dedicated to Krystle, my beautiful wife, soulmate, exploring partner and most of all, my best friend.

America Through Time is an imprint of Fonthill Media LLC
www.through-time.com
office@through-time.com

Published by Arcadia Publishing by arrangement with Fonthill Media LLC
For all general information, please contact Arcadia Publishing:
Telephone: 843-853-2070
Fax: 843-853-0044
E-mail: sales@arcadiapublishing.com
For customer service and orders:
Toll-Free 1-888-313-2665

www.arcadiapublishing.com

First published 2021

ISBN 978-1-63499-291-6

Typeset in Trade Gothic 10pt on 15pt
Printed and bound in England

CONTENTS

About the Author 4

Introduction 5

1 Benjamin W. Walker House 7

2 Hilltop Arms Apartments 14

3 Capitol City Motor Company 17

4 Capital City Cleaners 22

5 Empire-Rouse Laundry 33

6 St. John the Baptist Catholic Church 39

7 Grove Court Apartments 43

8 Sayre Street School 54

9 Governor's House Hotel 64

10 Penny Profit Meat Market 73

11 W. B. Paterson Elementary School 78

12 Koppers Industries Wood Treatment Facility 87

13 The Town of Spectre 92

ABOUT THE AUTHOR

David Bulit is a Hialeah native, a city within the greater Miami area, who has spent nearly a decade documenting abandoned locales throughout the state of Florida. Mostly known for his blog, Abandoned Florida, his photography has been featured by local, national, and international news outlets. His other published works include *Abandoned Jacksonville: Ruins of the First Coast*, *Lost Miami: Stories and Secrets of Magic City Ruins* and *Southern Comfort: Abandoned Homes of the American South*.

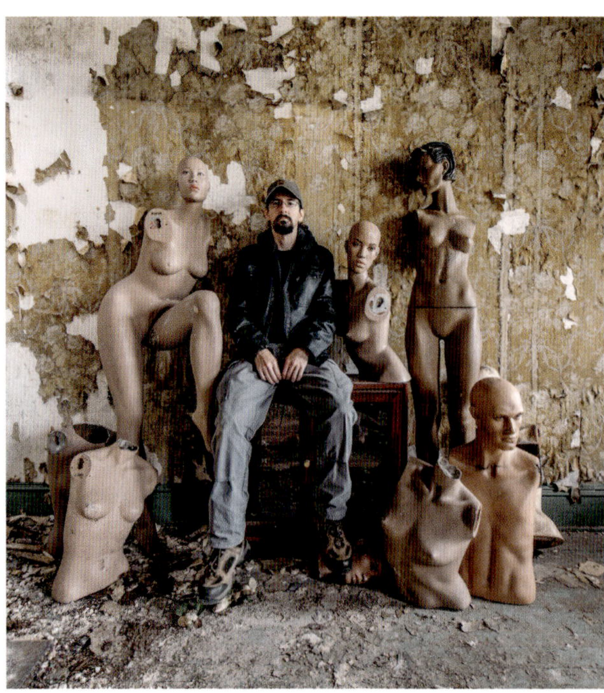

INTRODUCTION

Montgomery, Alabama, was incorporated in 1819 through the merger of two neighboring towns, Alabama Town and New Philadelphia. In 1846, the state capital was moved from Tuscaloosa to Montgomery as the city quickly grew due to its abundance of cotton crops and the back-breaking labor of the slaves who worked those fields. By that time, Montgomery had one of the largest slave markets in the South centrally located in Court Square, now nothing more than an old fountain. It would later become the site of many historical events that would change the country. One such event was the start of the American Civil War, when LeRoy Pope Walker, the Confederate States' secretary of war, sent a telegram from the nearby Winter Building in Court Square to General P. G. T Beauregard ordering an attack on Fort Sumter, starting the Battle of Fort Sumter and the beginning of the Civil War. When the Confederate States of America was formed in 1861, Montgomery was named the first capital of the nation, and Jefferson Davis was inaugurated as President on the steps of the State Capitol. A large wooden frame house built by William Sayre and later remodeled by the prestigious Winter family became the White House of Confederacy and executive residence of Jefferson Davis before the nation's capital was moved to Richmond, Virginia.

In the post-World War II era, African American veterans returning from the war were among the first on pushing to regain their civil rights in a segregated South. Famously, the Montgomery bus boycott was sparked after December 1, 1955, when Rosa Parks was arrested for refusing to give up her bus seat to a white man at Court Square. Court Square was not only once the place of the largest slave markets in the nation, but also the birth of the modern civil rights movement.

The following locations exhibit not only remnants of a segregated city, but the hardships citizens of Montgomery have endured, be it the loss of one's grand home;

two businesses which directly competed with each other only for both to ultimately go under; hotels and apartments blocks now home to the homeless; or an all-girls school seemingly forgotten and seen as contributing factor to the blight that blankets the city.

1

BENJAMIN W. WALKER HOUSE

The Benjamin W. Walker house on Goldthwaite Street is the best example of Queen Anne style architecture in the Cottage Hill District. The district was planned out in the 1830s by Edward Hanrick and is Montgomery's first and oldest historic district. It is situated on a low hill overlooking the Alabama River located just west of downtown. The district contains more than ninety houses constructed prior to 1910, most of which are simple frame residences with touches of Victorian and classical details. After the early years of the twentieth century, the city's more prominent families moved to the east along Court and Perry streets, leaving Cottage Hill to the middle and working class. Before the depression, several small cottages and apartments were constructed, and a row of small stores were built along Goldthwaite Street.

During the late 1950s and 1960s, the area declined and was slated to become an industrial warehouse complex according to the city's master plan. It wasn't until the 1970s that the area was recognized for its irreplaceable architecture and its potential as a downtown residential area. The district was placed on the Alabama Register of Landmarks and Heritage on April 16, 1975, and the National Register of Historic Places on November 7, 1976.

The district is surrounded by quite a few abandoned properties, but none are more impressive than the mansion that stands on Goldthwaite Street, considered one of the last examples of Queen Anne style of architecture in the area. Completed in 1896, it once belonged to Colonel Benjamin Winston Walker from Tuskegee, where his great-uncle General Thomas Woodward was one of the founders. Walker was a plantation owner, former Alabama Senator, and then appointed U.S. Marshall for the middle and southern districts of Alabama by President Benjamin Harrison, which prompted his move to Montgomery.

Walker was married to Josie Jerrol Alsop, the daughter of Thomas J. Alsop, a wealthy businessman who owned much of the land along Whitman and Goldthwaite Street. When her father died in November 1893, much of his estate, which included the property he owned, was left to his only child. It is speculated that around this time, the Walkers separated and the house was leased to a Montgomery judge.

When Benjamin Winston Walker died on December 30, 1907, the house was pillaged by his family, who removed the stained-glass windows and other valuables from the home. During the depression, it was converted into a boarding house, and this is when many of the alterations to the house occurred. Rooms were added on and the portions of the house were cut up in a way to allow more boarders to stay. According to a previous owner, there is even a staircase within one of the walls, blocked off during these alterations.

In later years, the house was bought by a man with the intention of renovating it and gifting it to his newly wed daughter and her husband. After a lot of demolition work, the project was abandoned and was sold away. The home was purchased by a couple in the 1980s who lived there for the next thirty years, restoring it and repairing the mistakes of previous owners. Many years later, the couple separated, just as Benjamin Walker and his wife did many years before. Despite having made substantial repairs and restoration work, a decision was made to sell the house, but only to someone with the intention of continuing to restore it, rather than having it demolished.

A local developer approached them numerous times offering to purchase the property, but was declined on every occasion. Finally, the home was purchased by a local woman under the guise of completely restoring the house to its former grandeur. In reality, the property was purchased under an LLC owned by the developer that had wanted to acquire it for so many years. This same developer had also purchased other properties in the area such as the Hilltop Arms Apartments and the former Capitol City Motors dealership. They planned on converting the old apartment building into a luxury boutique hotel with construction being completed by fall 2019. With no construction work occurring on the structure, the once lavish house on Goldthwaite St. now languishes in the shadow of the decaying remains of the Hilltop Arms Apartments.

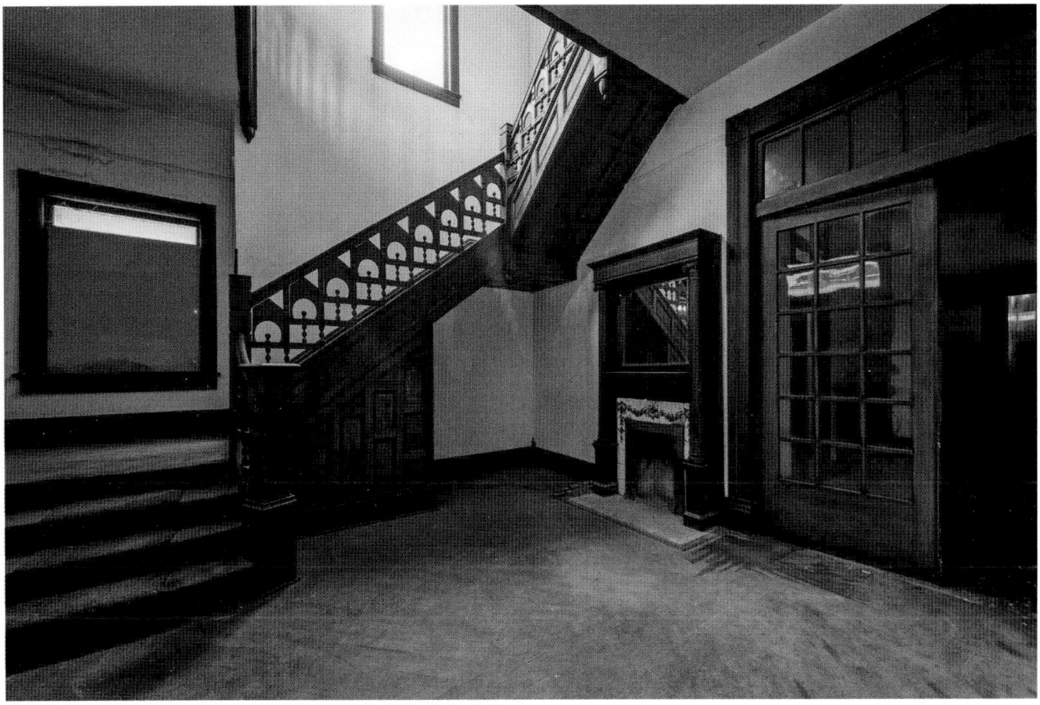

The staircase in the foyer is described as a masterpiece, with one owner wishing he had saved it before selling the property.

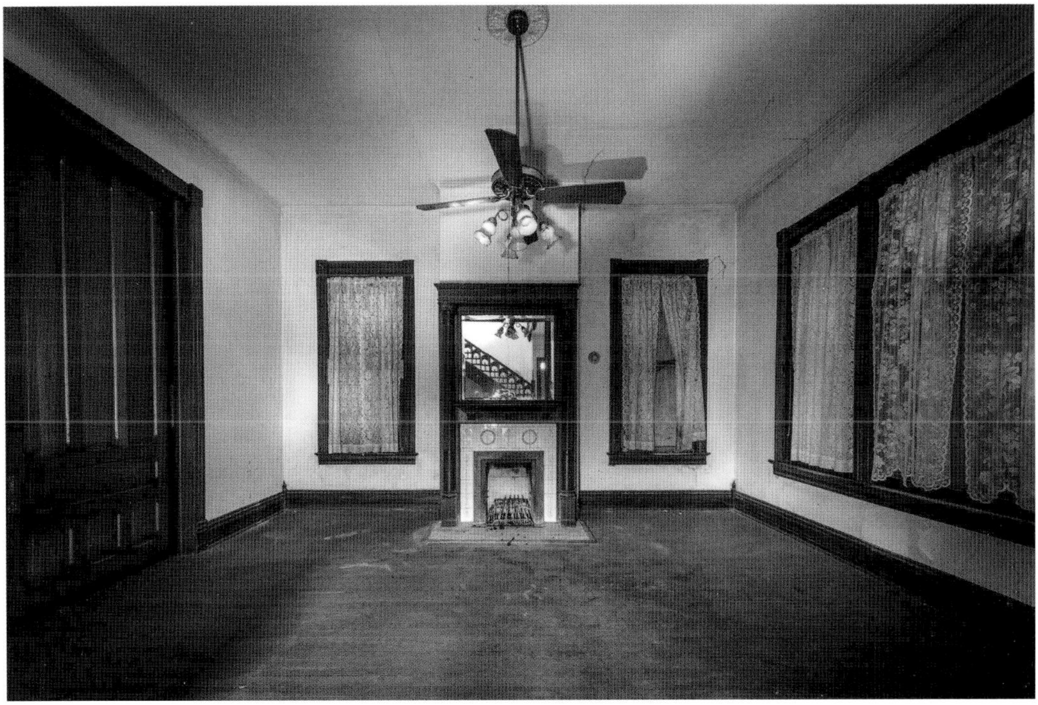

Historically known as a drawing room, the living room here was used to entertain many of Montgomery's higher-class citizens.

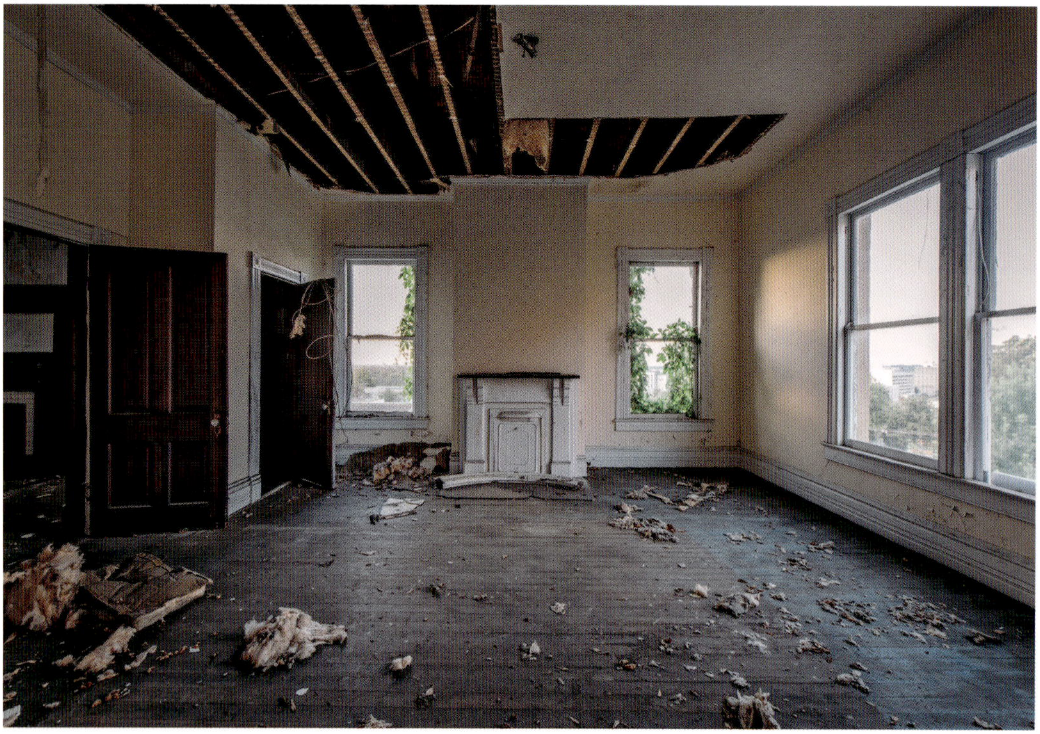

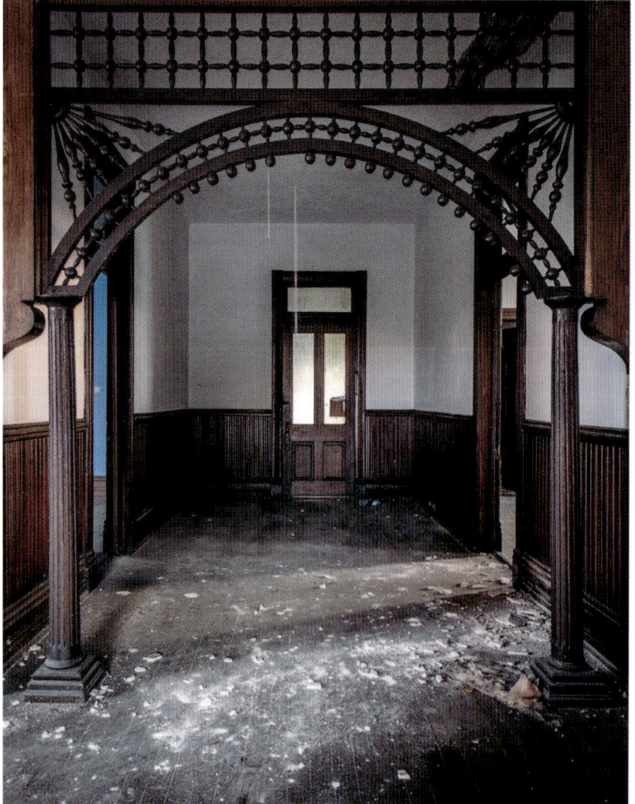

Above: A second floor bedroom, redone in later years as evidenced by the drywall

Left: An archway on the second-floor landing with a doorway at the end of the hall, which at one point probably opened into a bedroom, but no longer does.

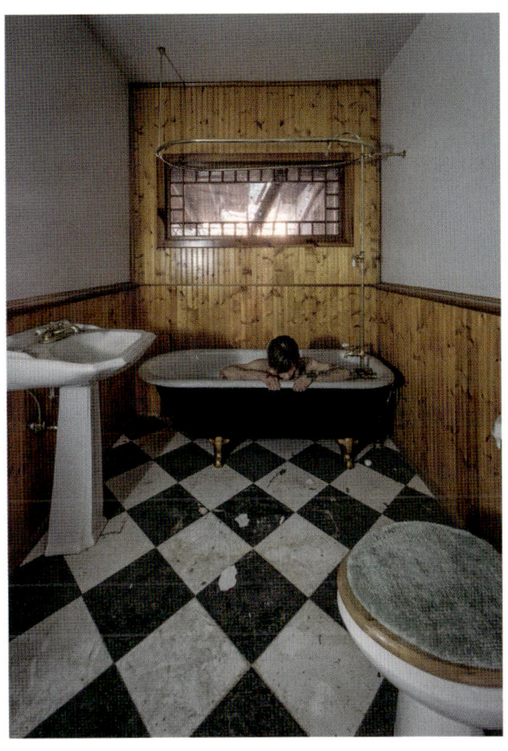

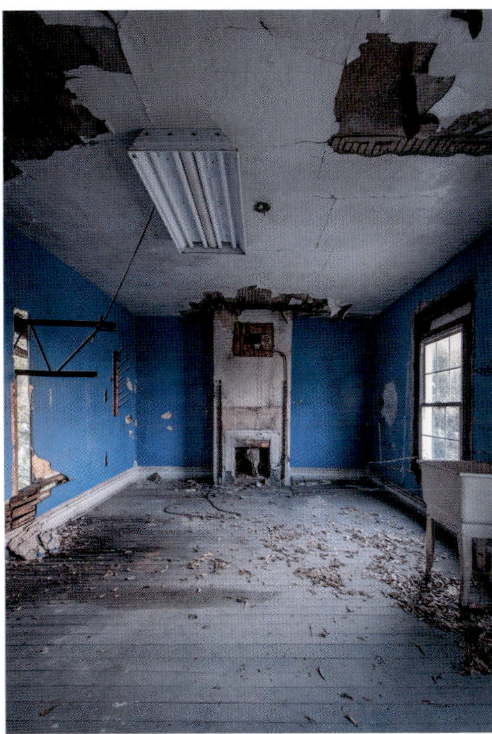

Above left: One of the many bathrooms in the house, this one being one of the more elegant ones.

Above right: A blocked-off bedroom towards the back of the house with the only entry being a small hole through drywall.

Right: Located on the second floor, the door on the right opens into nothing, as a staircase was probably located there at one point.

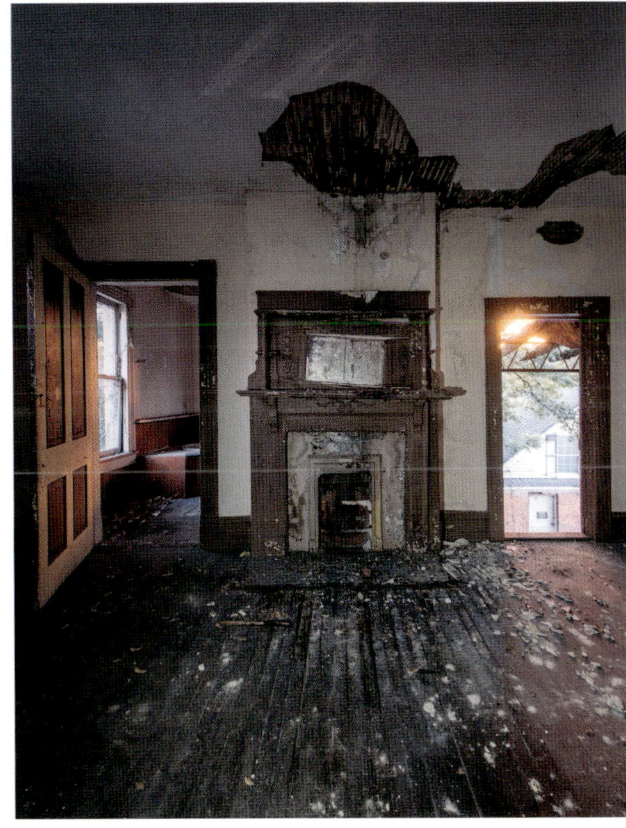

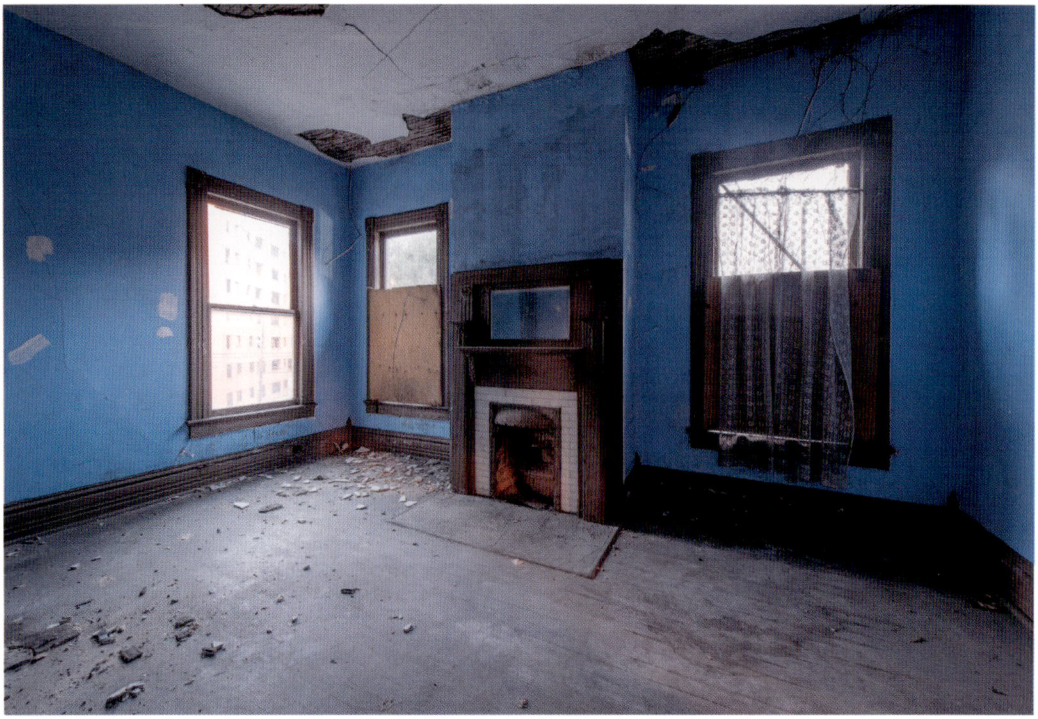

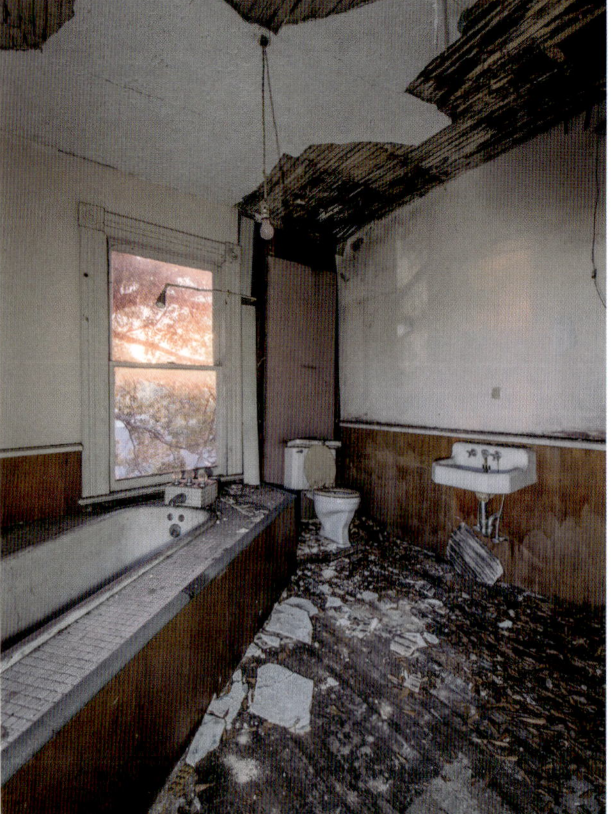

Above: Nearly every room in the house has a fireplace.

Left: A bathroom with a more modern tub and fixtures, probably added by the property's previous owner

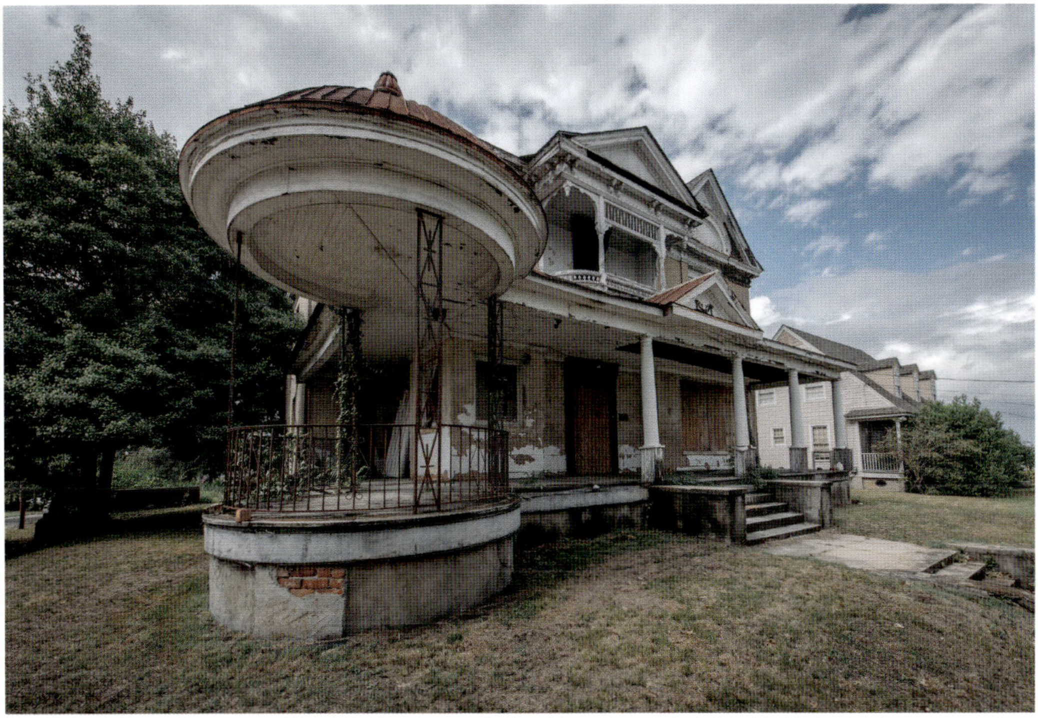

One of the notable features is the attached gazebo along the front of the house

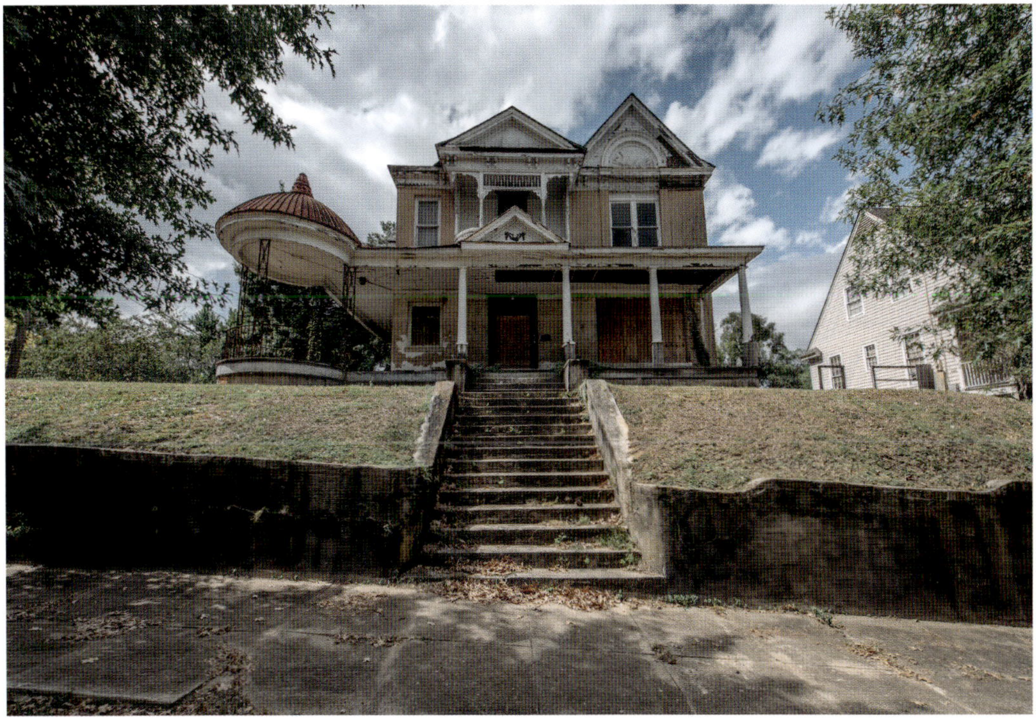

The Cottage Hill neighborhood where the house is located saw a decline in the 70s and 80s, but has recently seen a resurgence.

2

HILLTOP ARMS APARTMENTS

Located just on the outskirts of the Cottage Hill District are the remains of the Hilltop Arms Apartments building. Built in 1950, the building was designed by the architectural firm Pearson, Tittle, Narrows & Associates, known for their work on the Grove Court Apartments. The building contained 106 units as well as office space on the ground floor.

The building has been vacant for decades due to failed efforts to renovate it. In 2006, the Hilltop Arms Apartments building was purchased by Kim F. Henderson for $787,000, who, by spring 2014, had dumped $1.4 million into the property. He blamed legal issues and the mortgage crisis for abandoning his development plans, adding that a low rental rate in the city was keeping new investors away from the project. The City of Montgomery offered Henderson $25,000 for the property with plans to demolish the building and prepare the site for the fiftieth anniversary of the Selma-to-Montgomery March. Such a low offer, it's no surprise that it was declined.

In 2016, a local developer purchased the property with plans to turn the vacant building into an upscale boutique hotel. The Hilltop Suites & Spa was to feature eighty suite hotel rooms, more than 6,000 square feet of meeting and event areas, and numerous bars and restaurants, including a rooftop bar and lounge overlooking Montgomery's downtown area. The developer also considered adding mixed-use space to include shops, grocery stores, and residential units. Other properties were purchased around the structure, including the nearby Benjamin W. Walker House as part of the project. Construction was to begin in spring 2018 with work expected to be completed by fall 2019.

Years later, the building remains empty with no substantial work done to the building. The decaying remains of the Hilltop Arms Apartments looms over the city's downtown and Cottage Hill District, a reminder of the blight throughout the city of Montgomery.

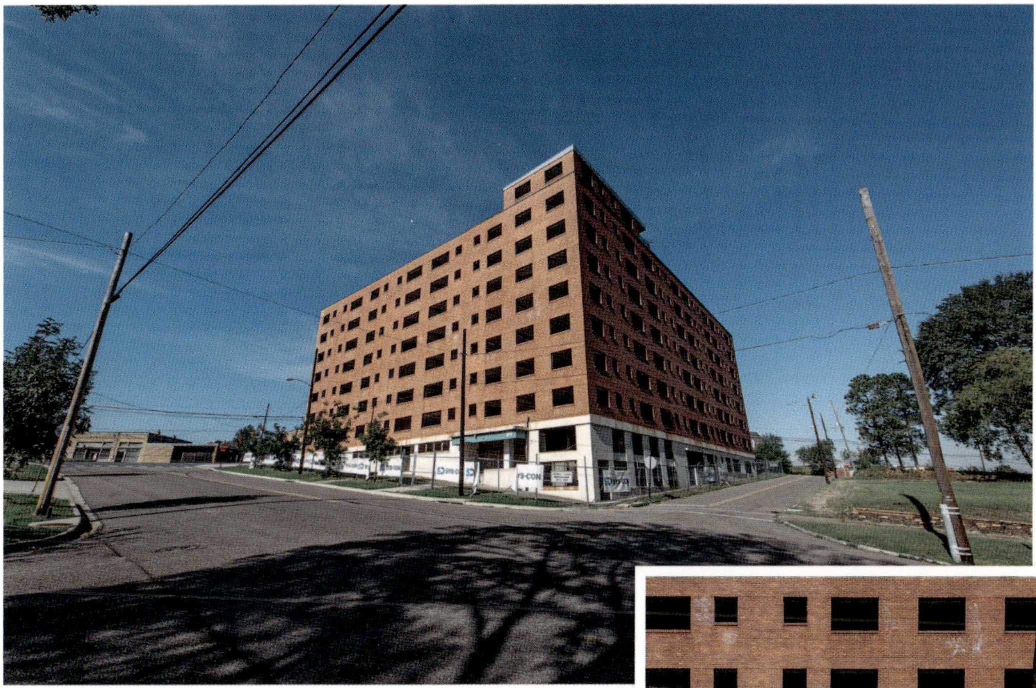

The enormous Hilltop Arms Apartments were designed by Pearson, Tittle, Narrows & Associates, known for their work on the Grove Court Apartments. *Right:* The entire interior of the building has been gutted down to bare concrete.

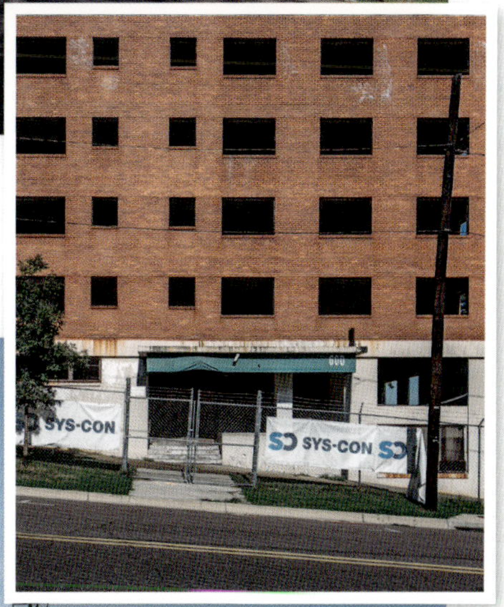

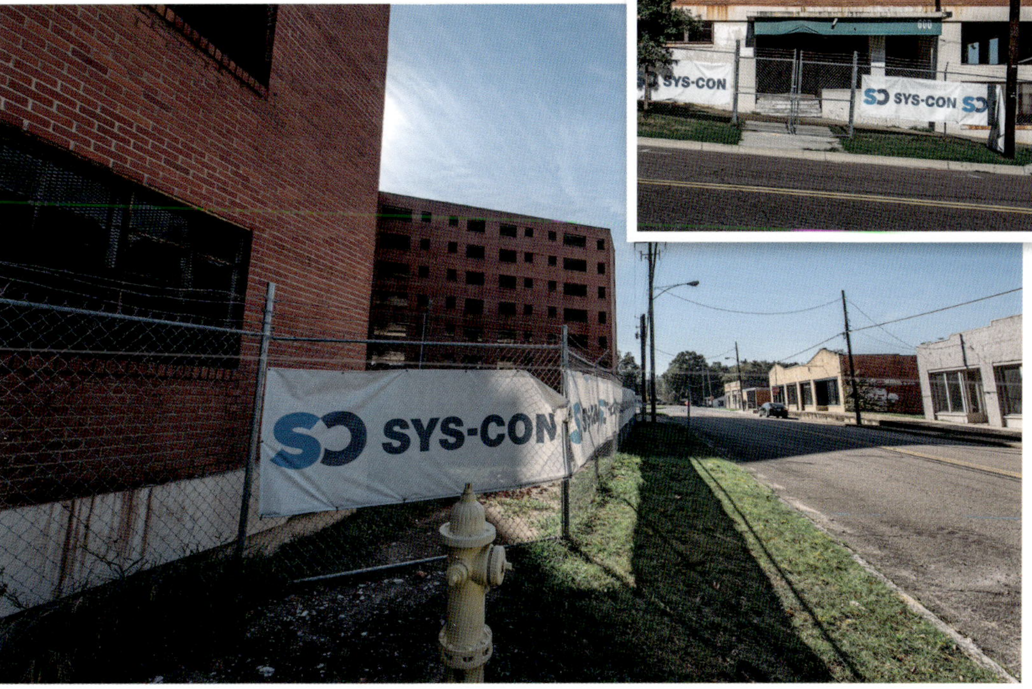

Fencing and signs remain as if construction is to begin at any moment.

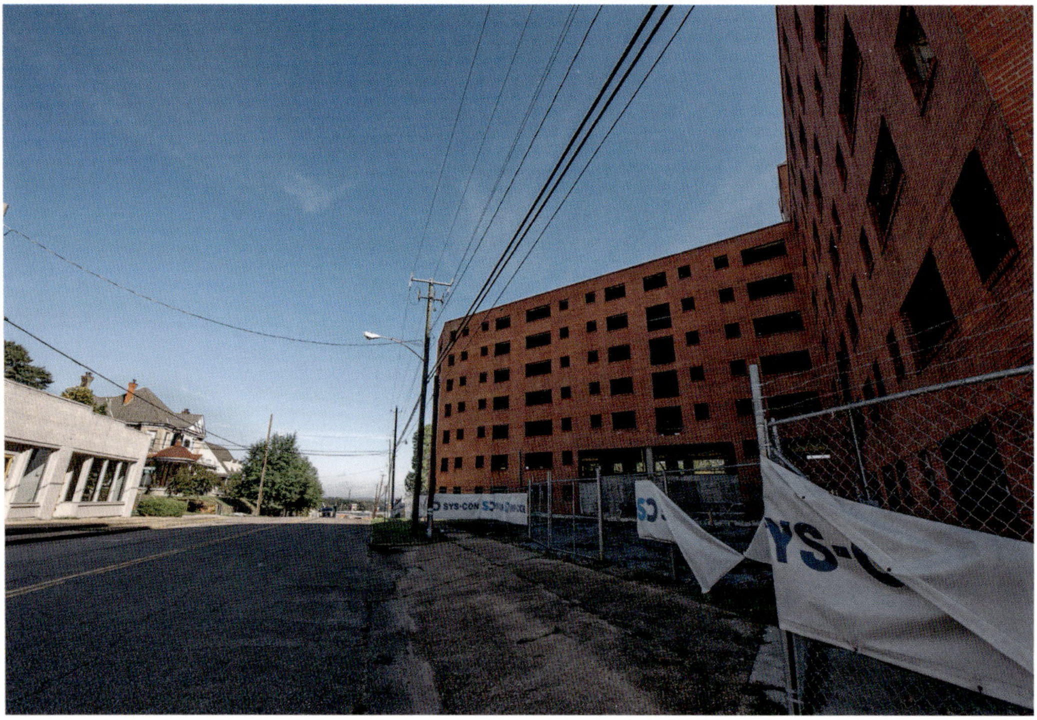

The B. W. Walker House can be seen on the left towards the back.

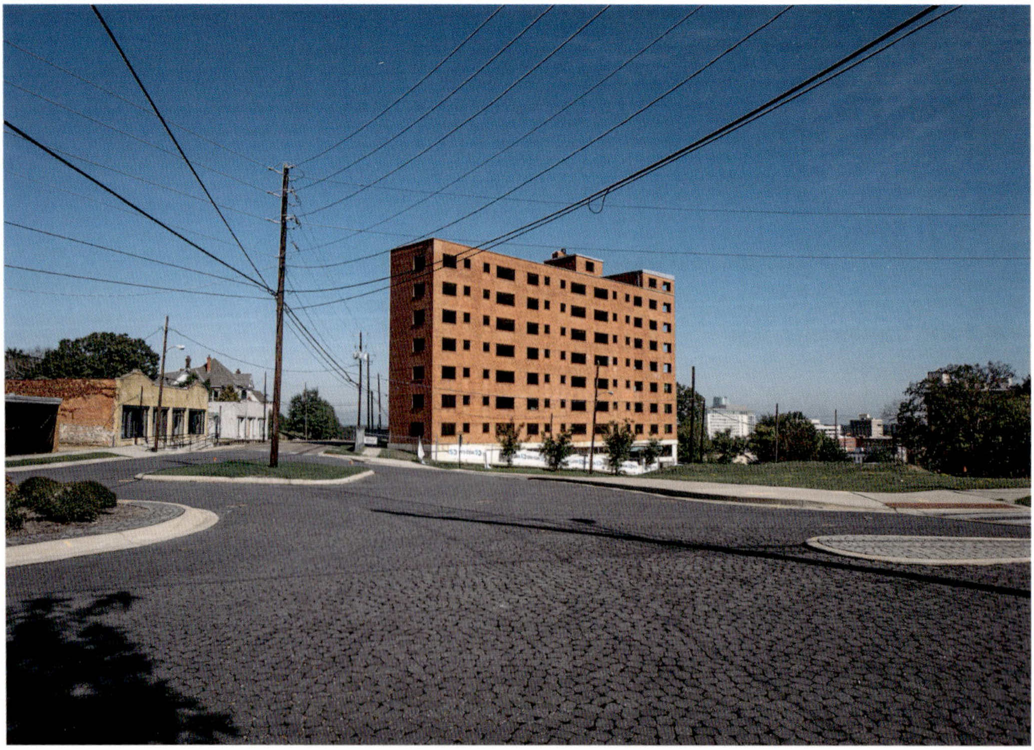

This portion of Cottage Hill is largely vacant due to failed promises and lost business.

3

CAPITOL CITY MOTOR COMPANY

The Capitol Motor Company showroom was built in 1950 on the corner of Goldthwaite and Herron just on the outskirts of the historic Cottage Hill District in Montgomery. The company competed with the Grimes Motor Company located just a couple of blocks north, though while Grimes Motor Co. sold Ford trucks and vehicles, Capitol Motor Co. sold Oldsmobiles. Unfortunately, the business closed down in the early-1970s as the area declined.

In later years, an antique shop moved into the building directly importing fine eighteenth, nineteenth, and twentieth-century antique French furniture and decorative accessories. In October 2018, the building was purchased by local developer Sys-Con LLC, mentioned earlier as the owner of the Hilltop Arms Apartments and the Benjamin W. Walker house.

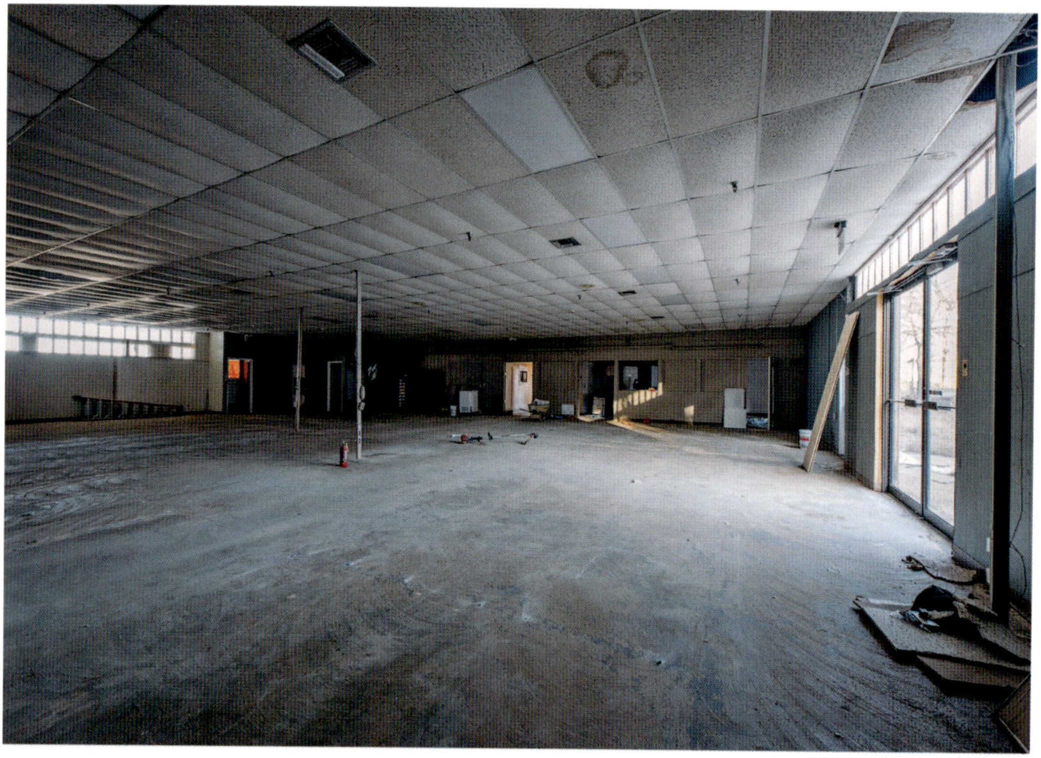

The empty warehouse just behind the small showroom.

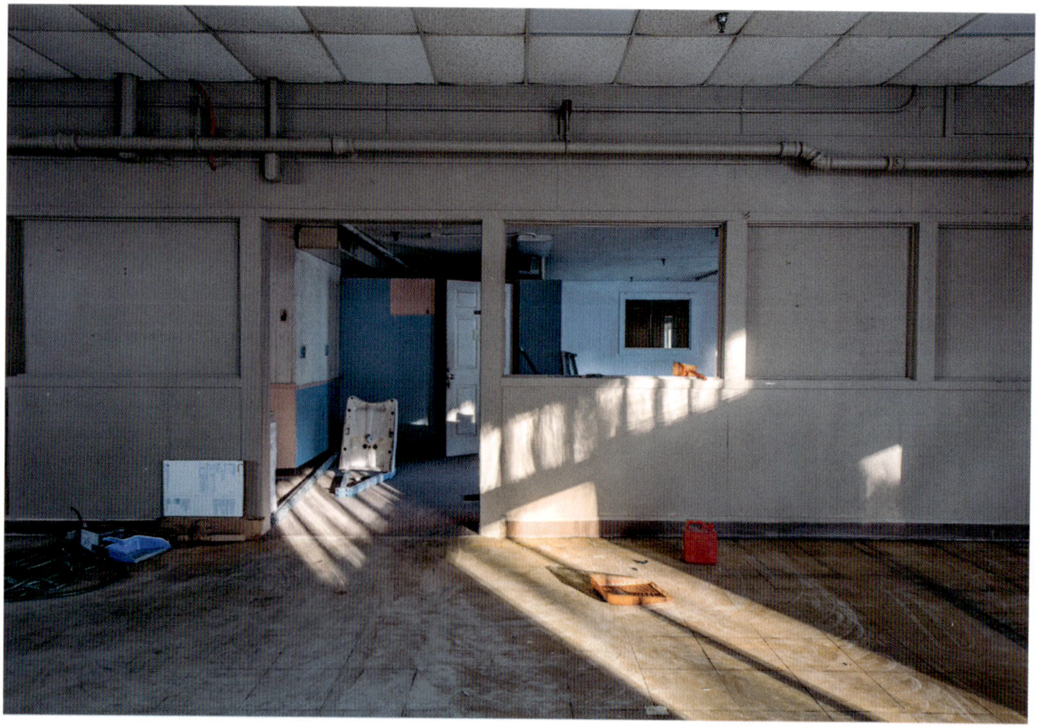

There seems to have been work done throughout the building, which was halted before it was finished.

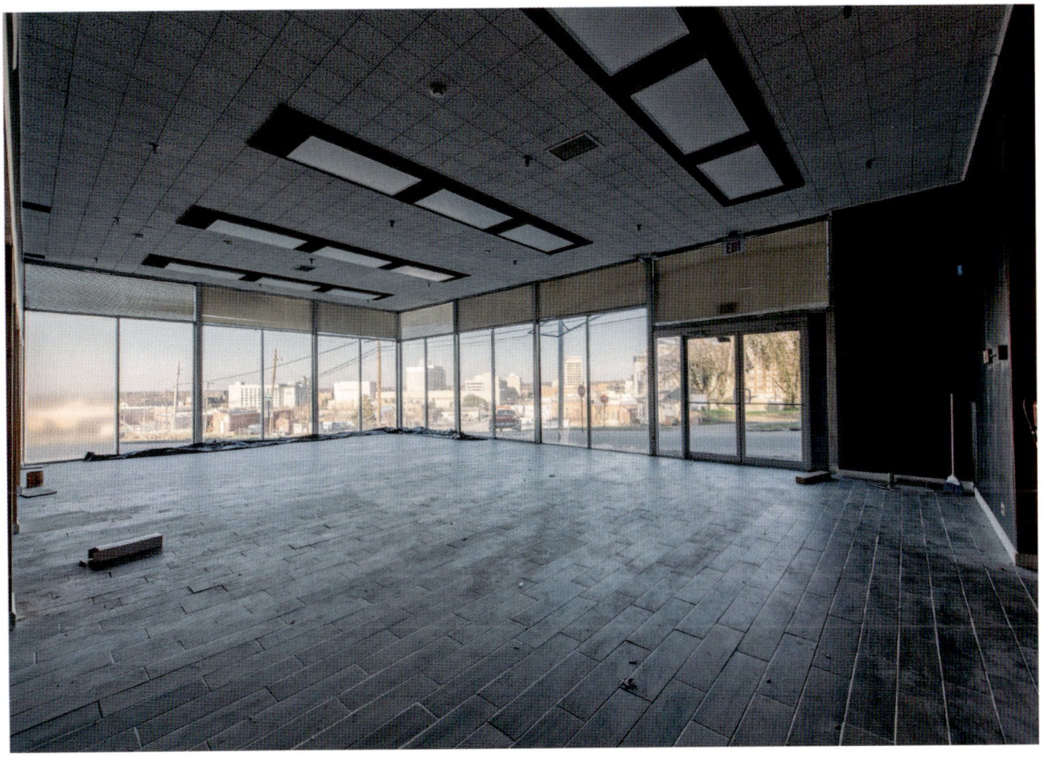

Inside the showroom looking out towards the corner of Herron and Goldthwaite Streets.

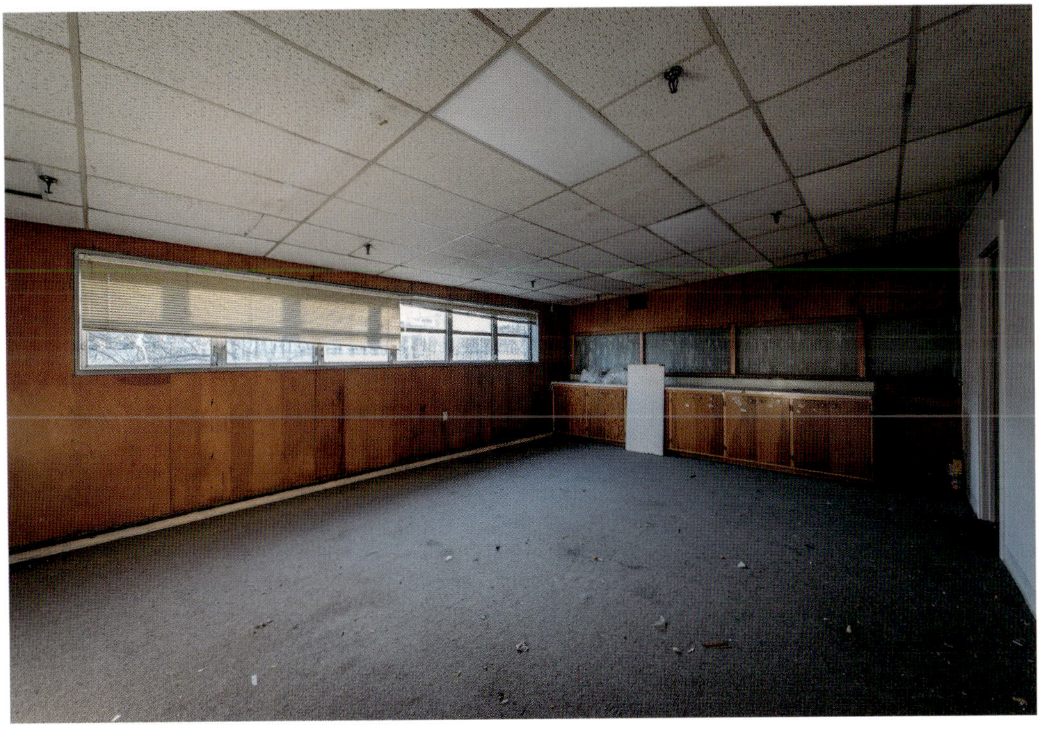

An office with wood paneling, a common sight during the 80s and 90s.

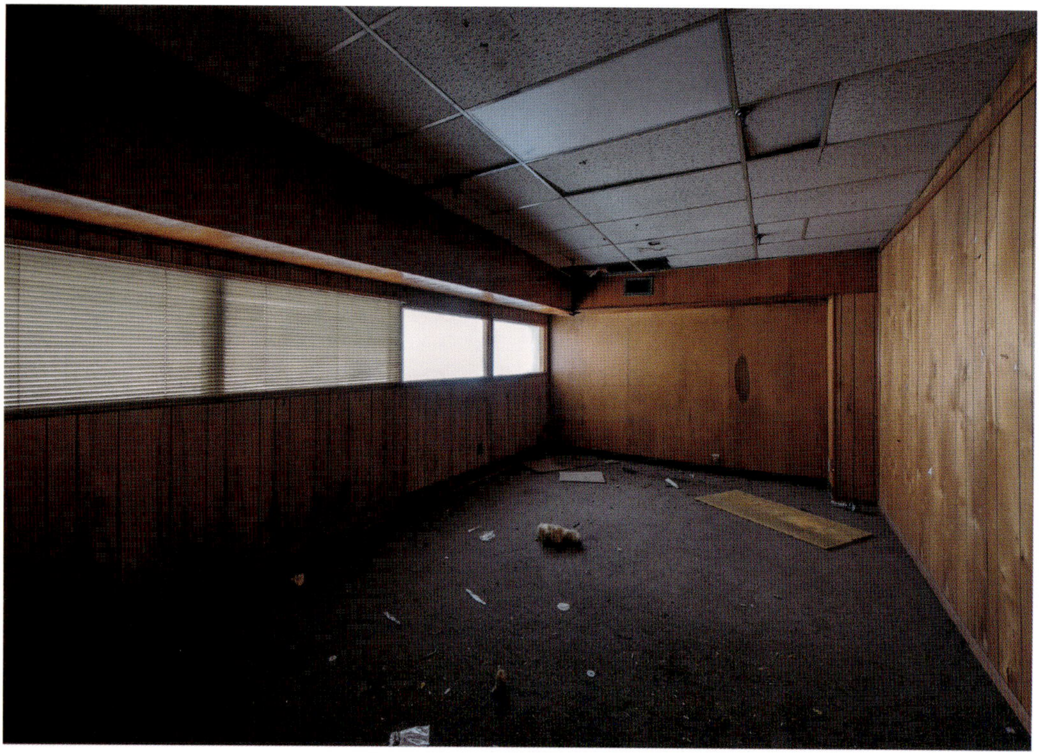

A small meeting room with a view of the office space next door.

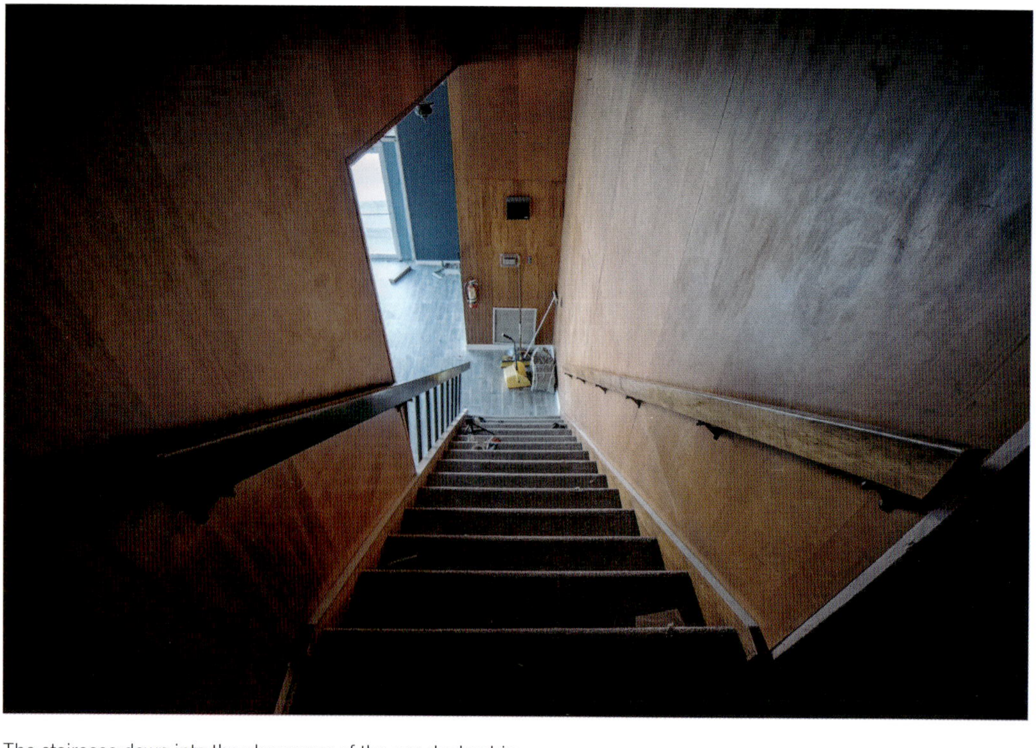

The staircase down into the showroom of the car dealership.

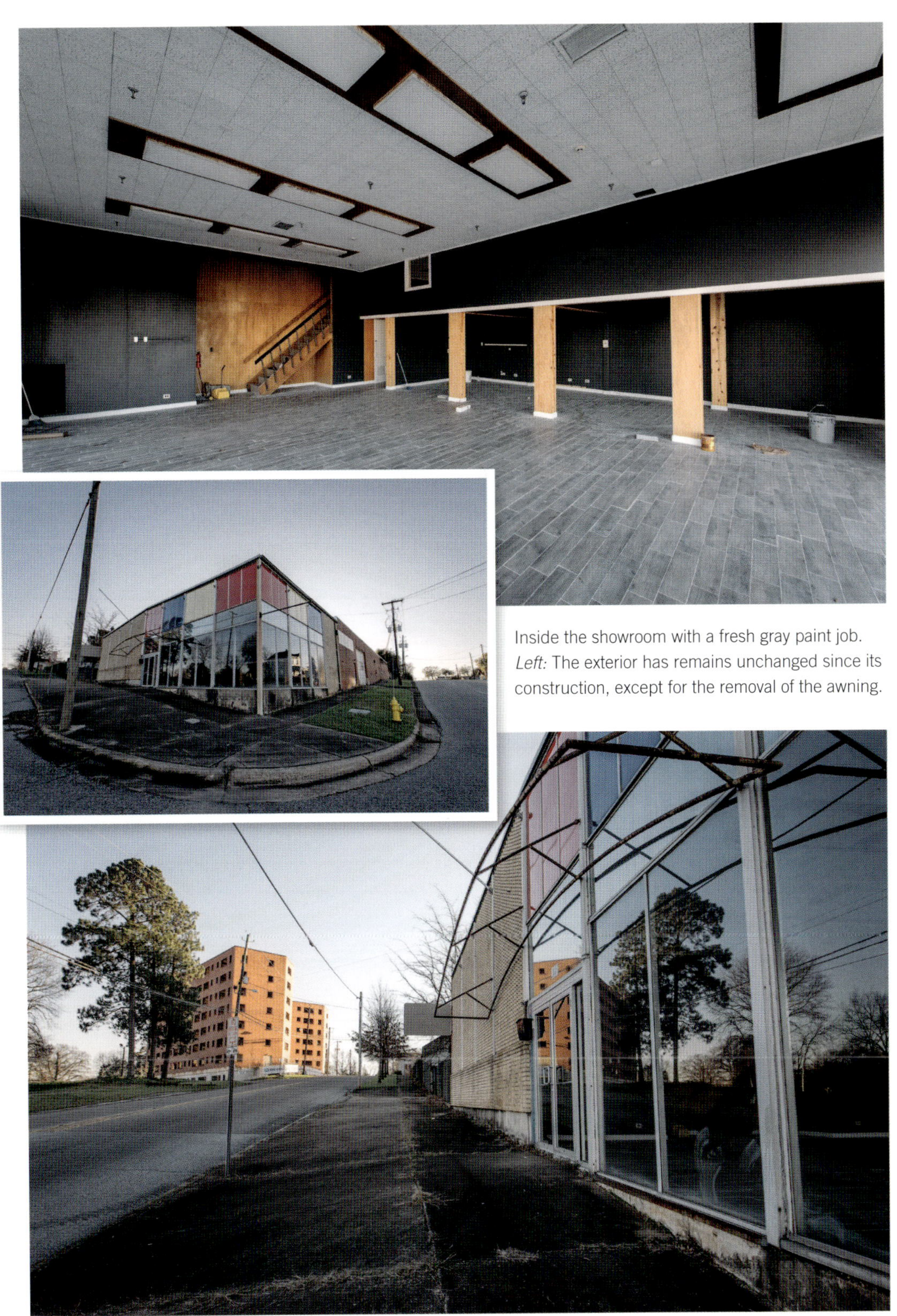

Inside the showroom with a fresh gray paint job.
Left: The exterior has remains unchanged since its construction, except for the removal of the awning.

The Hilltop Arms Apartments can be seen just down the street.

4

CAPITAL CITY CLEANERS

Capital City Laundry was founded in 1893 by Charles Milton Smith, Sr. His son, Charles Milton Smith, Jr, modernized the business and built the current building across from their competitor, Empire-Rouse Laundry, which operated out of a red-brick building. His son, Charles Milton Smith III, would later join his father in the family business.

Empire-Rouse was founded sometime in the early twentieth century with L. D. Rouse as part owner. Empire-Rouse differed from Capital City Laundry by offering a "family wash," which meant an entire family's clothes were all washed together for a low price. Later on, the business would switch to coin-operated machines. By the 1950s, his son-in-law, Clement Tranum Fitzpatrick, would be running the business as well as the Governor's House Hotel on South Boulevard, among others.

At its height, Capital City boasted eleven locations throughout the city of Montgomery while Empire-Rouse only had eight. Capital City Cleaners ran advertisements against their competitor claiming the "family wash" that Empire Laundry touted was inadequate as loads of clothing would become mixed and employees regularly wore their customers' clothing. The current Capital City Cleaners location was renovated in 1959 in order to compete with the neighboring Empire-Rouse, dominating the smaller business in sheer size alone. But as the years went by, other competitors were established, one being Davis Cleaners, which moved into the old Empire-Rouse building in 1981. Capital City continued on well into the new millennia.

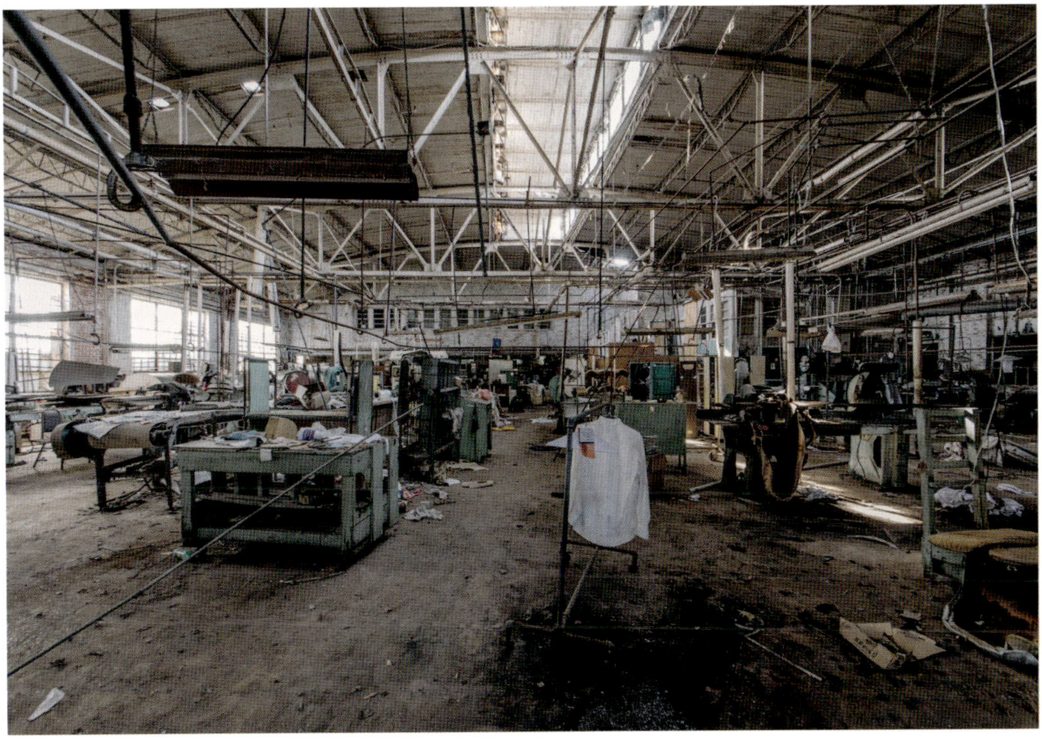

Tons of equipment and clothing was left behind at the former Capitol City Cleaner flagship location.

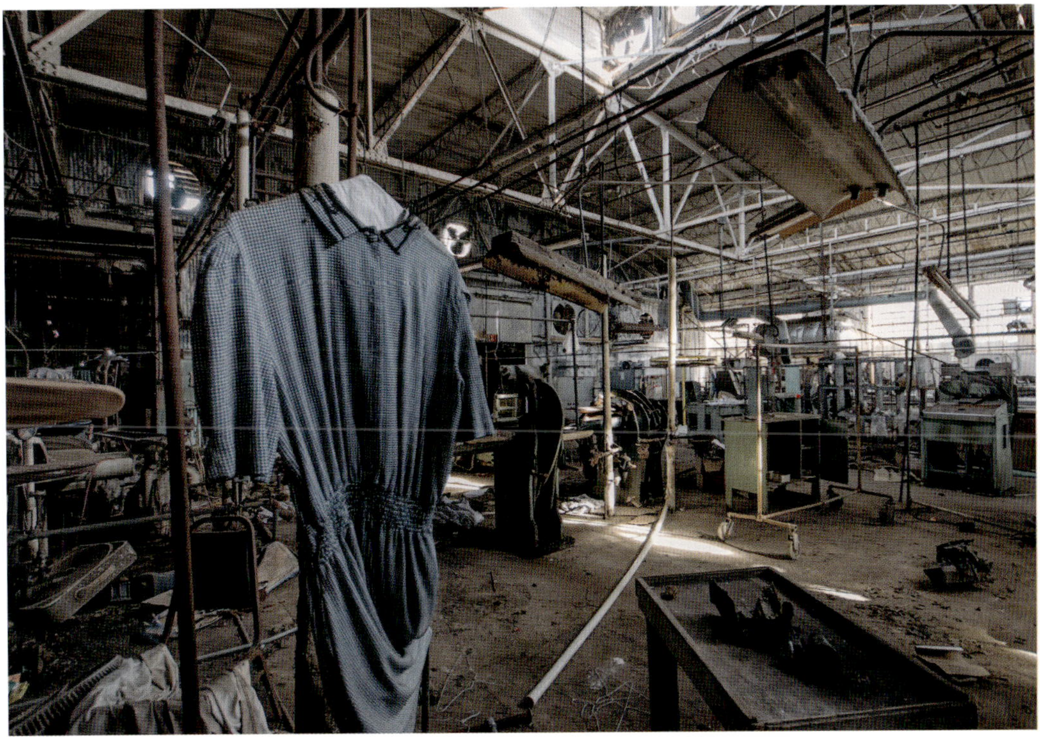

All the clothing in the building was vintage dating back from the 1970s, some dating back to earlier.

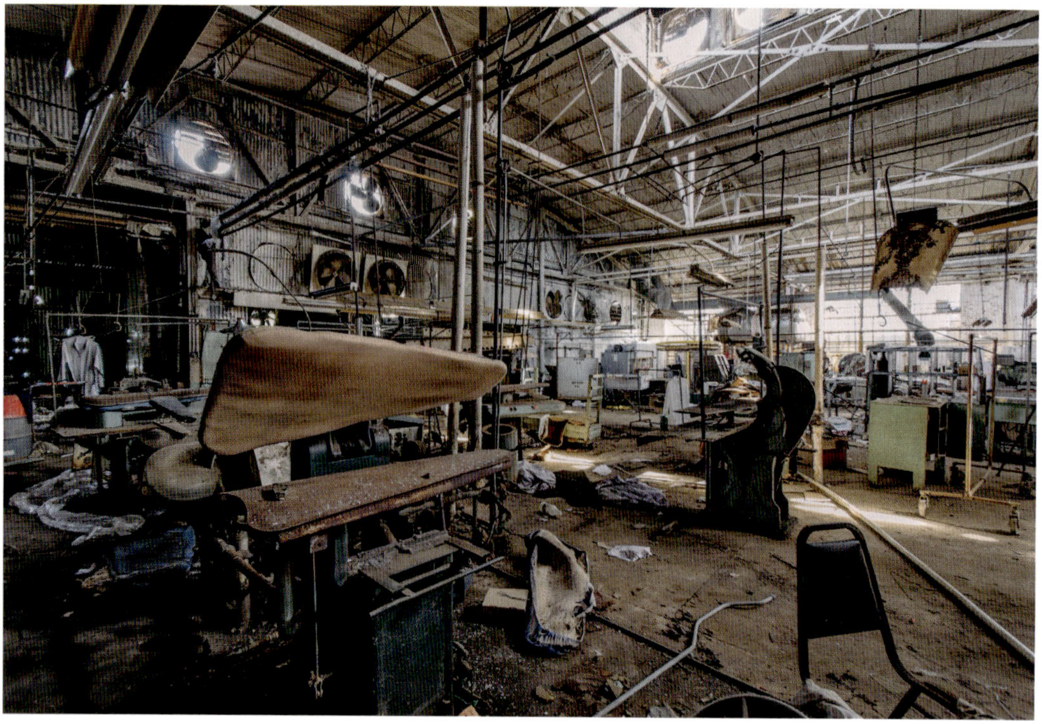

A steam press to iron out clothing quickly and efficiently.

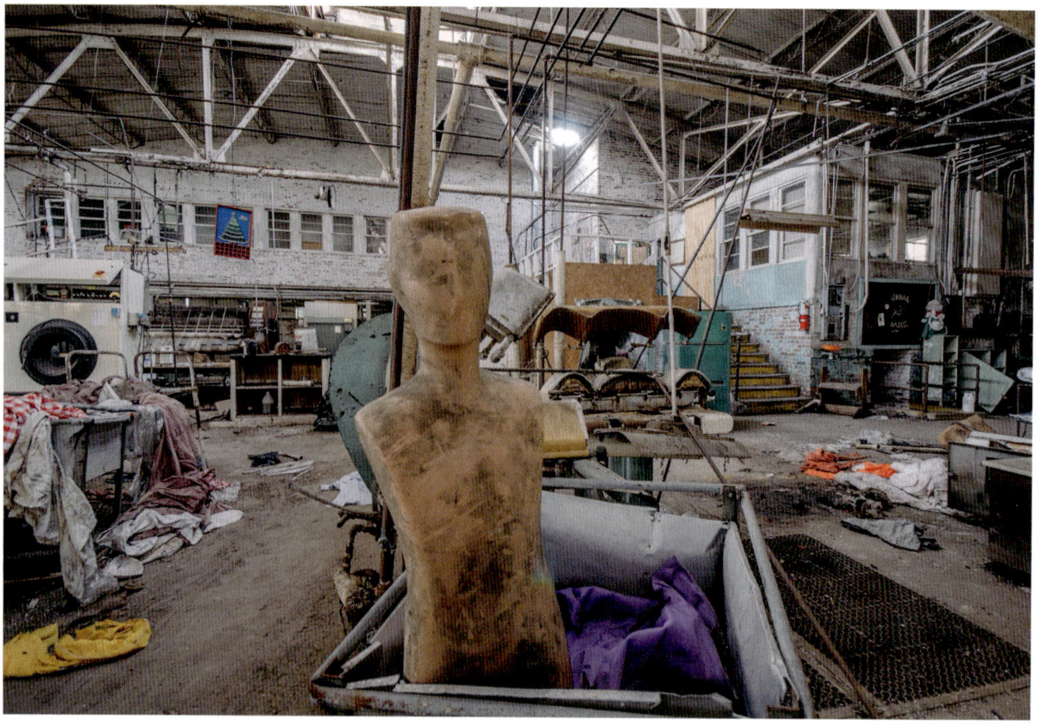

A dummy is among all the stuff left behind when Capitol City Cleaners closed.

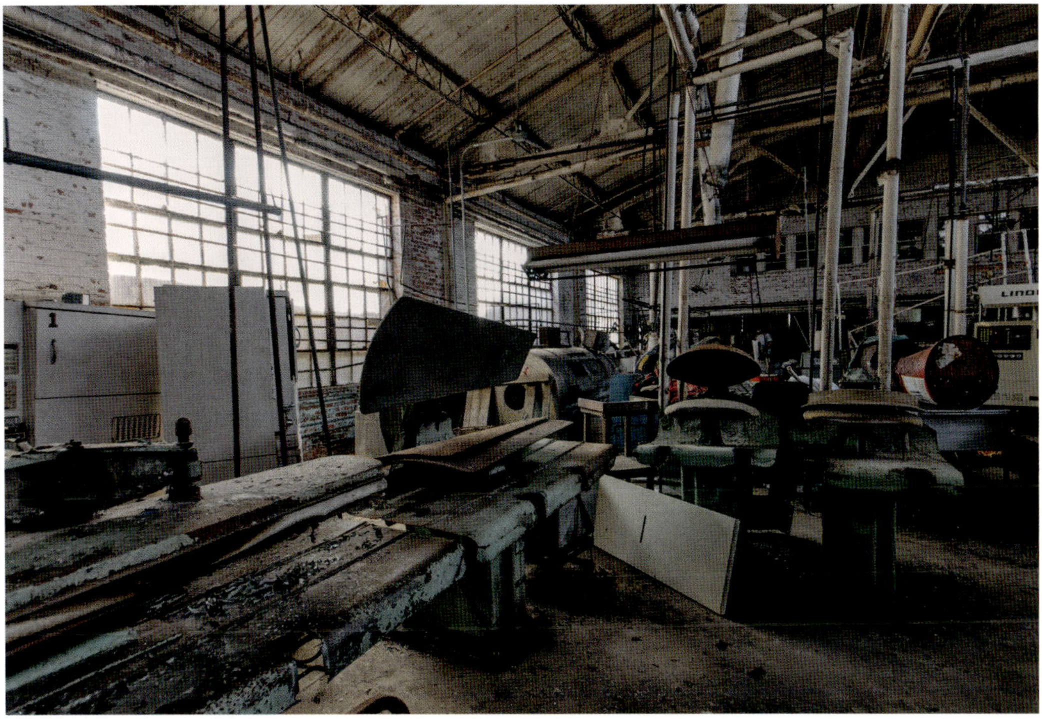

These steam presses give an idea how these dry cleaners were run like an actual factory.

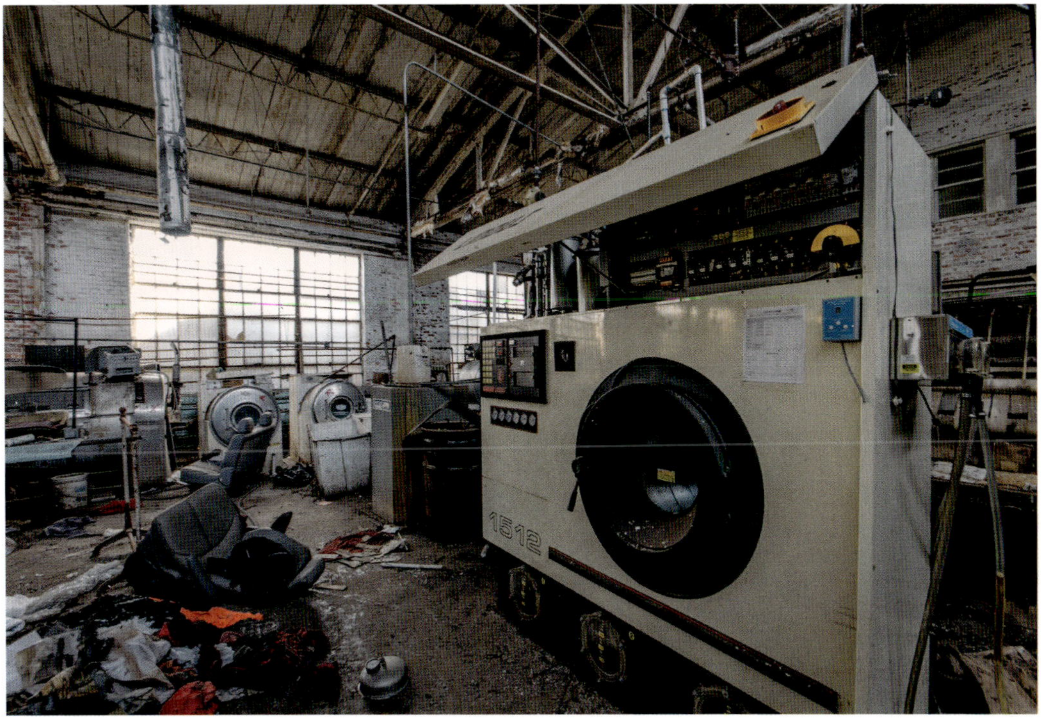

This industrial-sized washing machine has probably seen hundreds of thousands of articles of laundry pass through it.

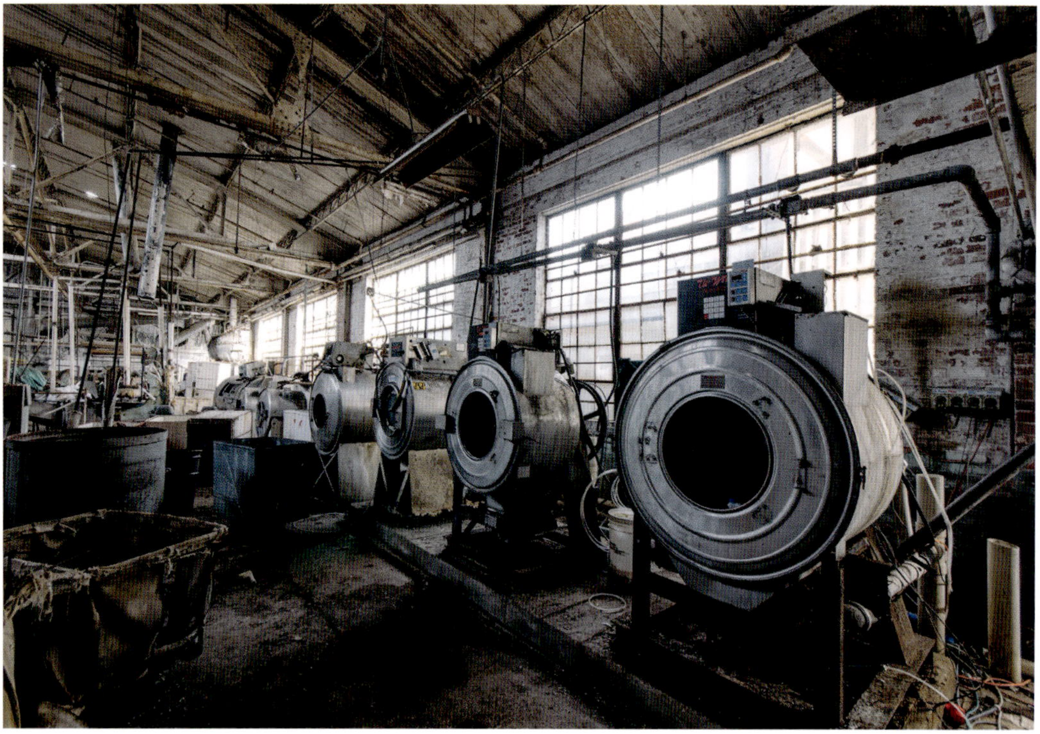

Multiple industrial-style washing machines.

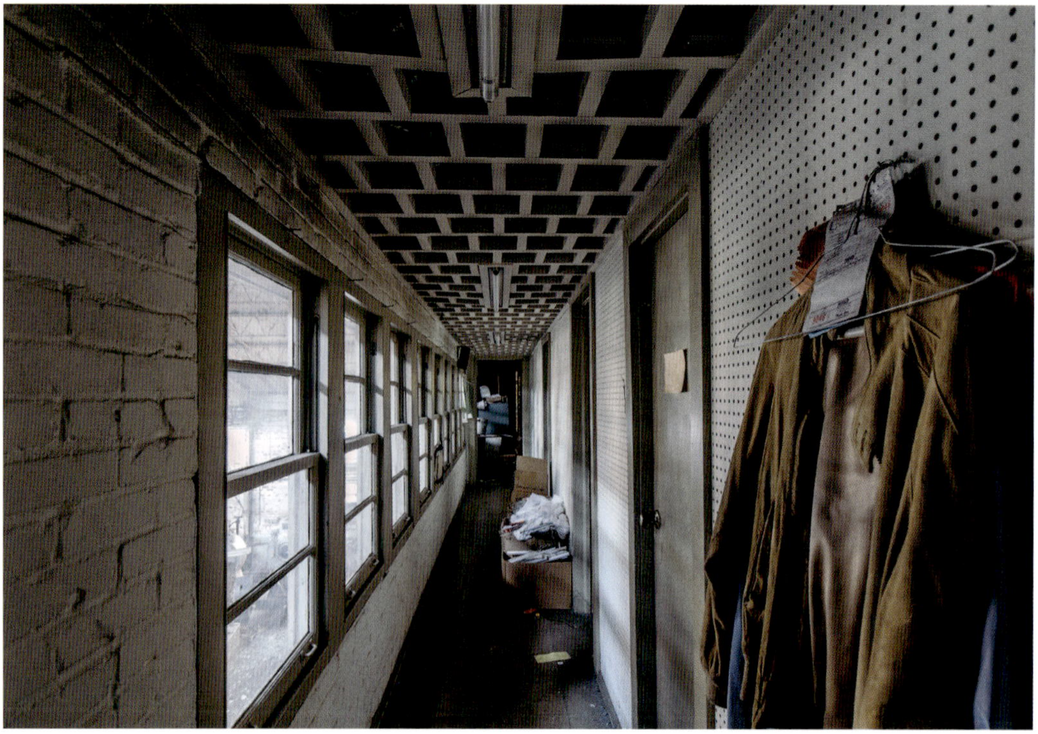

The hallway to the management and accountant offices.

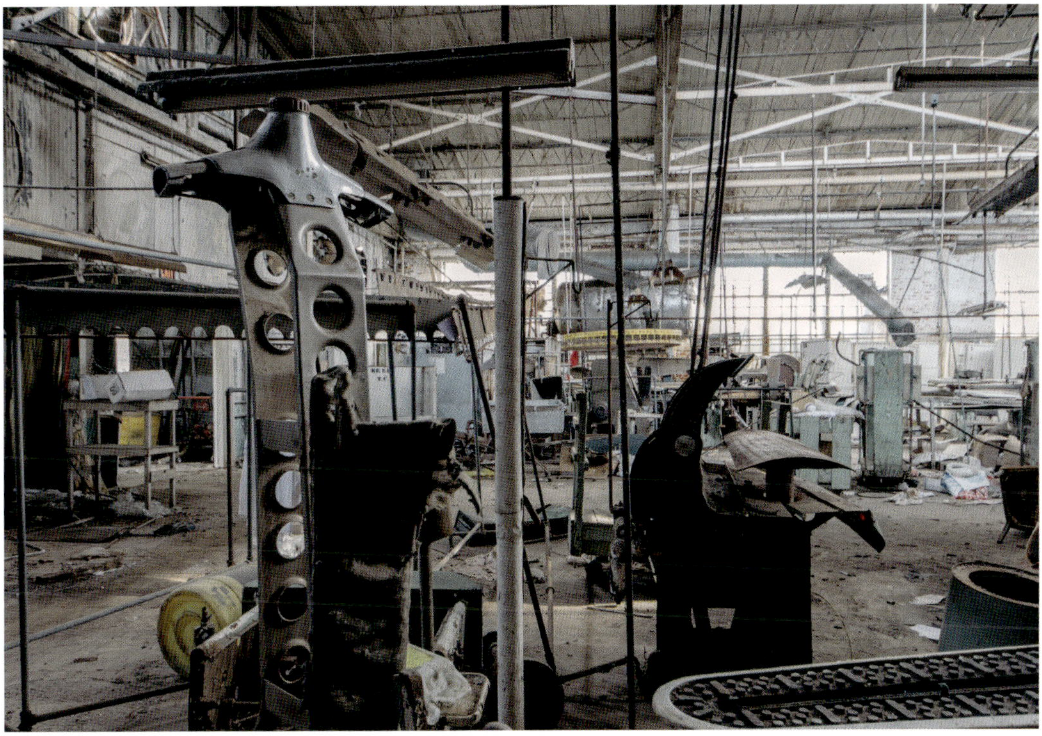

Although a lot of the equipment is worth quite a bit of money, they sit rotting away in the shuttered building.

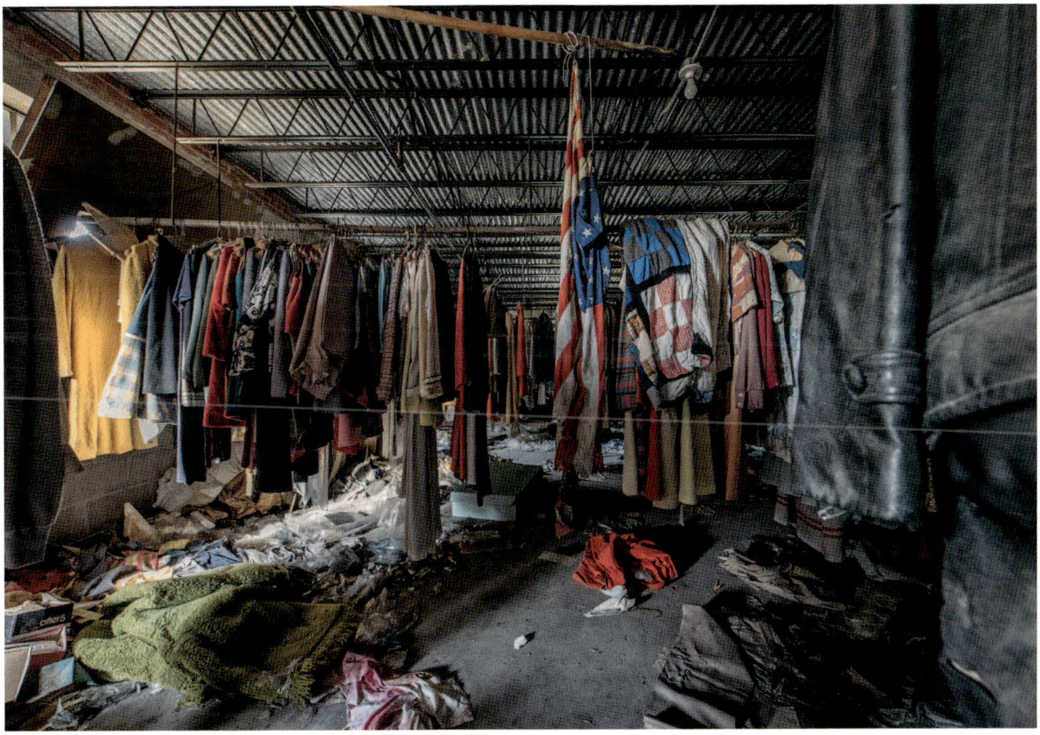

A dirty, soiled American flag hangs from a rusted pipe.

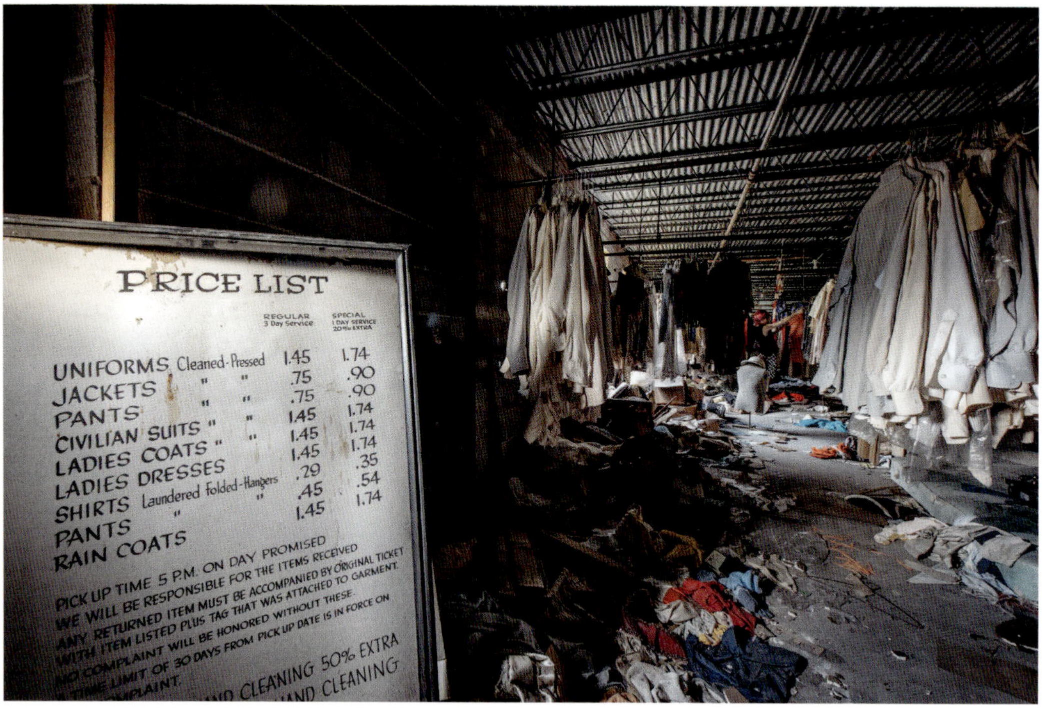

This pricing list was used around the 1960s and 70s.

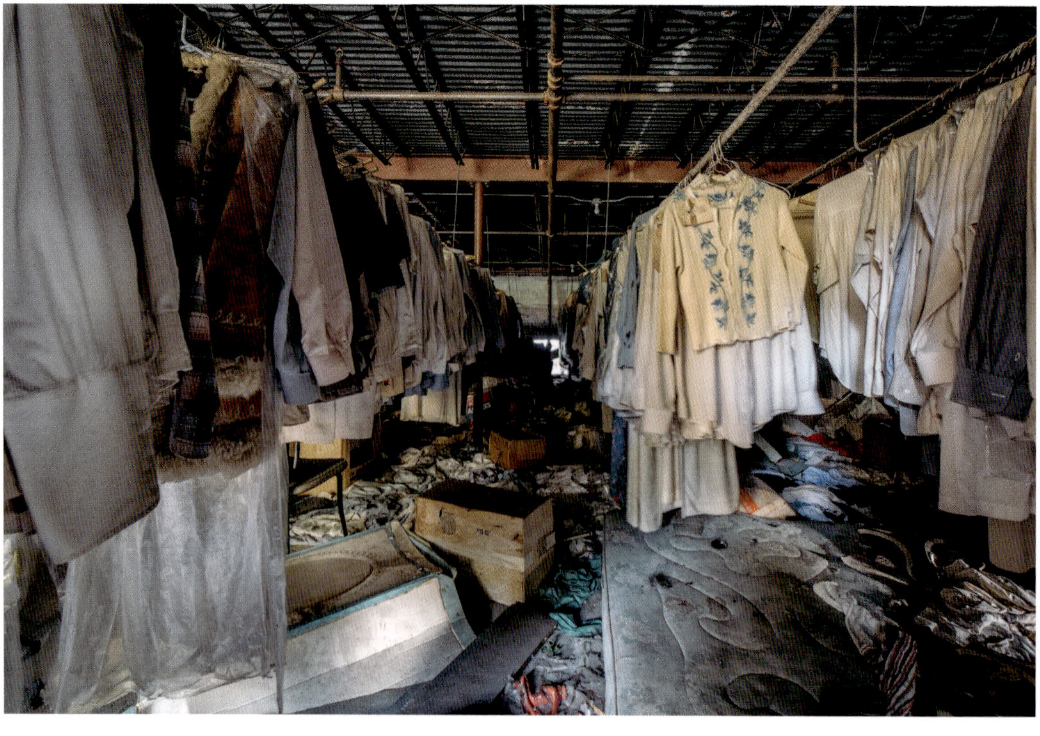

Much of the clothing here is so damaged and decayed that they fall apart with a soft tug.

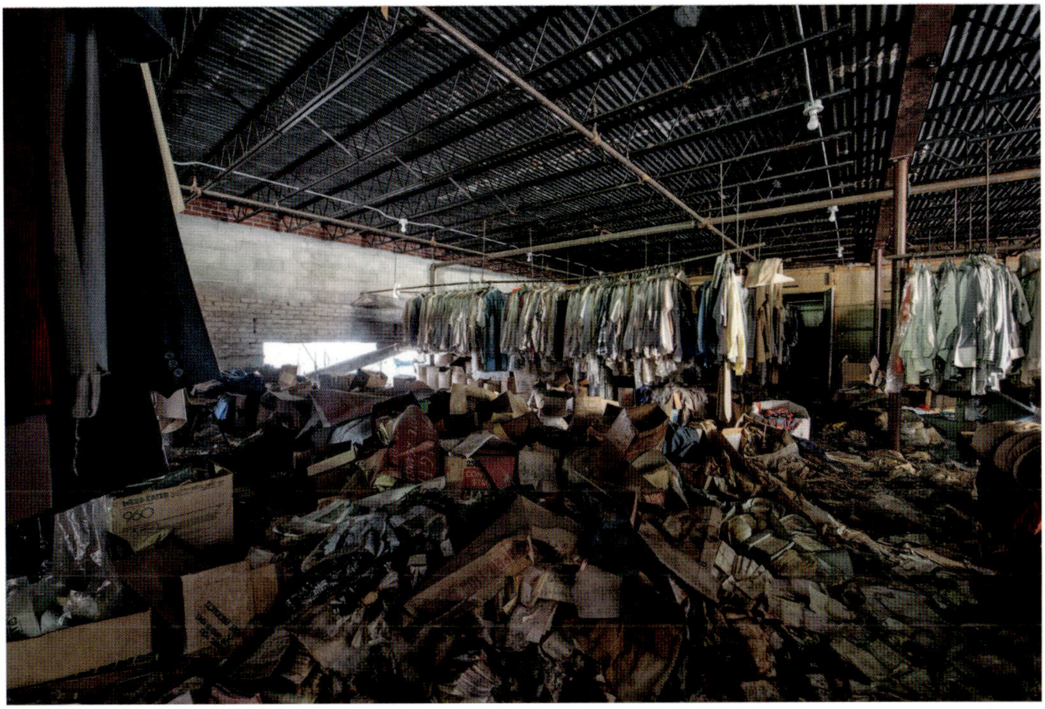

Mountains of dirty clothing, with some sitting on the damp floor so long, they've become nothing more than masses of black gunk.

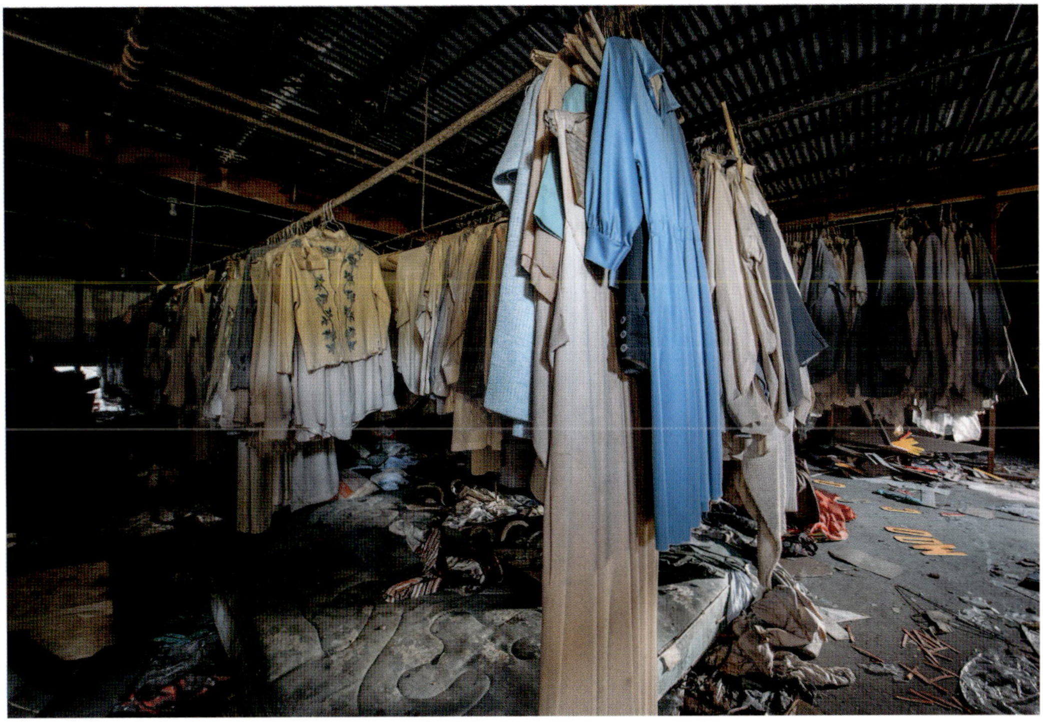

Homeless people frequently used the old building as shelter

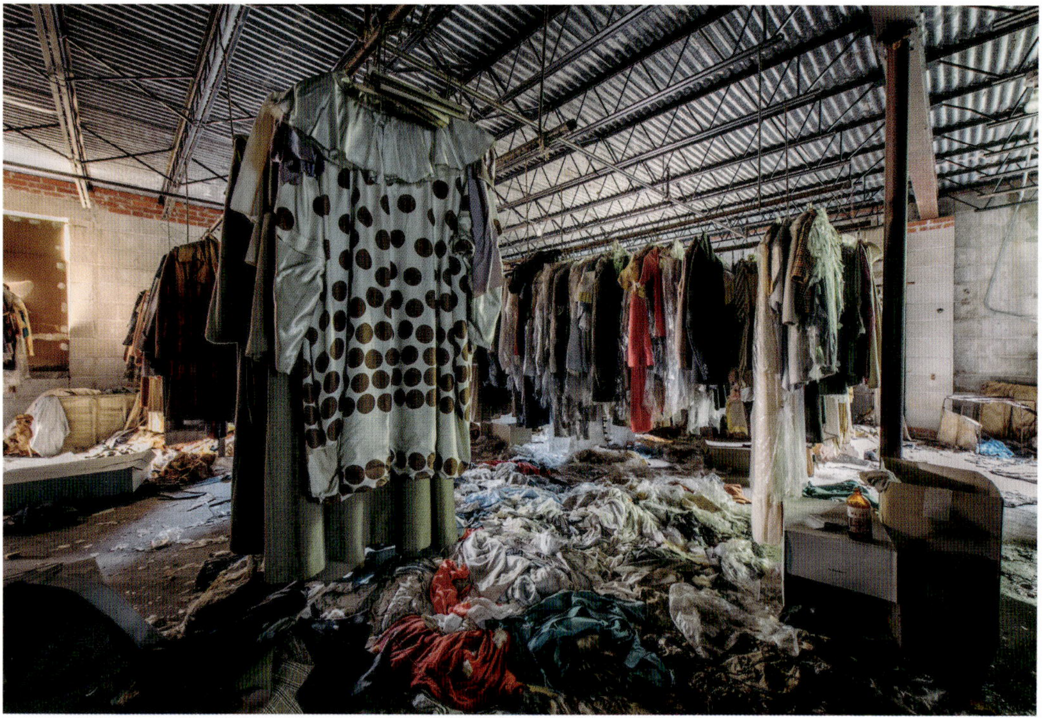

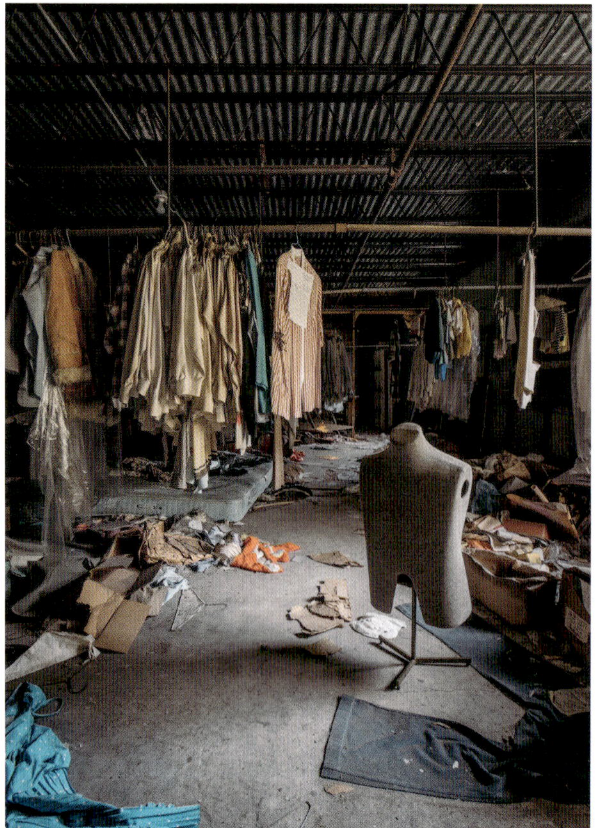

Above: A vintage clown costume hangs among thousands of articles of clothing.

Left: This dressmaking dummy probably made repairing clothing much easier.

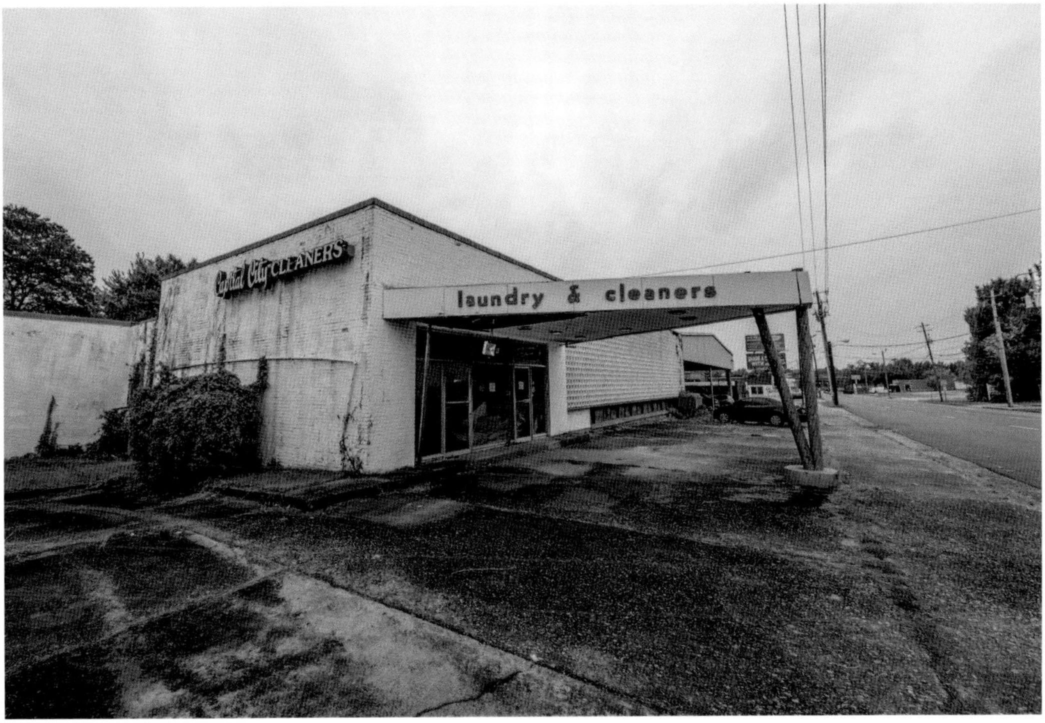

Above: The building received a much needed facelift in 1959 to compete with the neighboring Empire-Rouse Laundry.

Right: The lettering on the side of building is faded and falling apart.

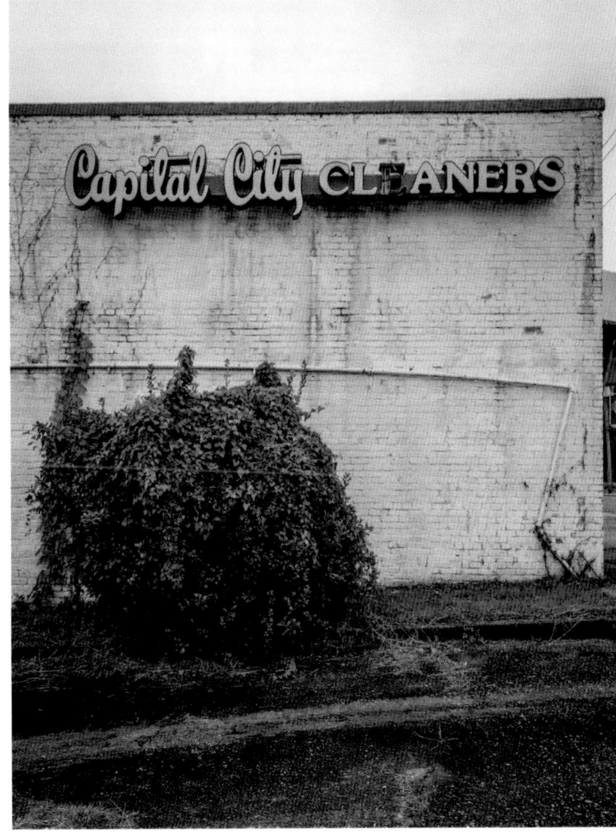

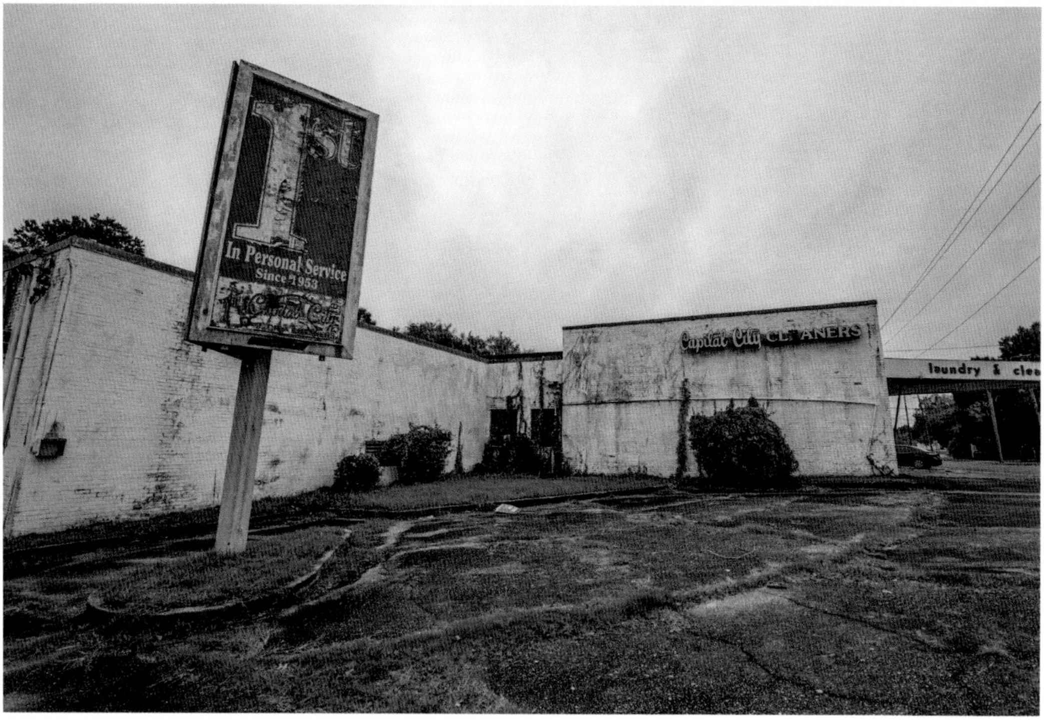

Capital City Cleaners has been at the location since 1953.

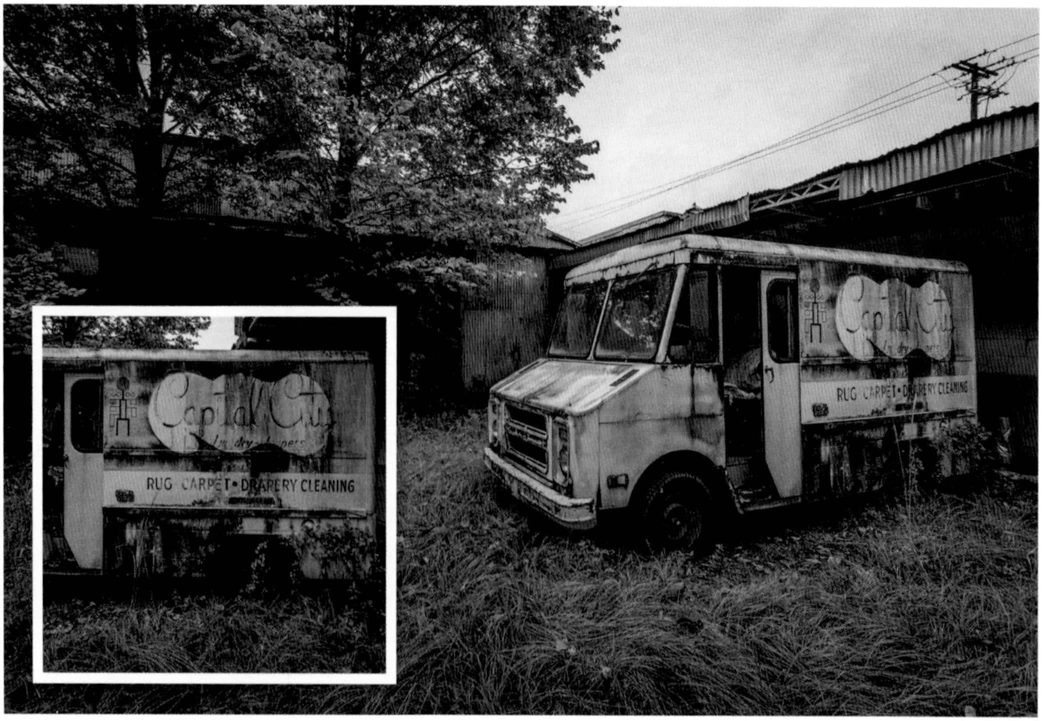

An old laundry delivery truck wastes away hidden behind the building among the weeds and tall grass. *Inset:* A close-up of the signage on the side of the old laundry delivery truck.

5

EMPIRE-ROUSE LAUNDRY

Empire-Rouse was first founded sometime in the early-twentieth century as Empire Laundry with L. D. Rouse as part owner. Empire Laundry advertised themselves as being able to wash an entire carload of laundry for the low price of 10 cents a pound. This was possible with the use of "floating roll" machinery made for ironing clothing. L. D. Rouse spent $10,000 to have it installed and touted it as being the second of its kind in the South.

L. D. Rouse passed away on May 27, 1957, and his son-in-law, Clement Tranum Fitzpatrick, took over the business. C. T. Fitzpatrick attended Sidney Lanier High School, and the Marion Military Institute in Marion, Alabama, where he would serve on the Board for thirty-eight years. He served in World War II as an officer in the U.S. Navy and was honorably discharged with the rank of lieutenant. Afterward, he enrolled in the American Institute of Laundering in Joliet, Illinois, where he joined his father-in-law in the family business.

C. T. Fitzgerald was quite a successful businessman having not only owned Empire-Rouse Laundry, but also the Governor's House Hotel on South Boulevard, as well as having a hand in developing Governor's Square Shopping Center and Gladlane Estates. He was one of the founders of Thermal Components and one of the founders of Guilford Company. He was also a partner in Moody Tire Company and in Natural Gas Appliance Company.

At its peak, Empire-Rouse boasted eight locations with their main location on Decatur St. Their main competitor was Capital City Cleaners, which boasted over eleven locations. They had their main building just across the street, and later expanded operations to the current structure which stands today. By the 1950s, Empire-Rouse had become nothing more than a coin-operated laundromat. As more competitors were established around the city of Montgomery, Empire-Rouse could not keep up with the competition and eventually closed down. In 1981, another laundry business, Davis Cleaners, would move into their main location on Decatur St.

In 1993, the Capital City Plume was discovered when construction workers discovered contaminated groundwater during the construction of the RSA Tower energy plant. The Environmental Protection Agency (EPA) got involved in the late 1990s and suggested that the Capital City Plume be put on the National Priorities List (NPL) and officially labeling it as a superfund site.

The city of Montgomery managed to avoid having most of its downtown area labeled a superfund site by taking full responsibility for its cleanup. The Downtown Environmental Alliance was created, consisting of multiple state government agencies whose responsibility was the planning and the cleanup costs of the site. These actions have become an example of how a city should proceed with cleaning environmental disasters and highly polluted areas.

After years of testing, the EPA concluded that the contamination of the groundwater was most likely caused by the commercial printing industry that resided in downtown Montgomery in the late-1800s and early-1900s, mainly the *Montgomery Advertiser*. The *Montgomery Advertiser* challenged the accusations with their own tests, concluding that the contamination was caused by nearby gas stations and the chemicals used by dry cleaners.

Some businesses continued operating as normal as the city's aquifer was determined to have not been contaminated. Many businesses weren't so lucky as a high amount of crime, low quality of life, and a shrinking population has caused businesses to close down. The cleanup of the Capital City Plume is an ongoing effort still to this day as well as the city's ever-growing blight problem, which both Empire-Rouse and Capital City Cleaners became a part of, falling victim to the plume.

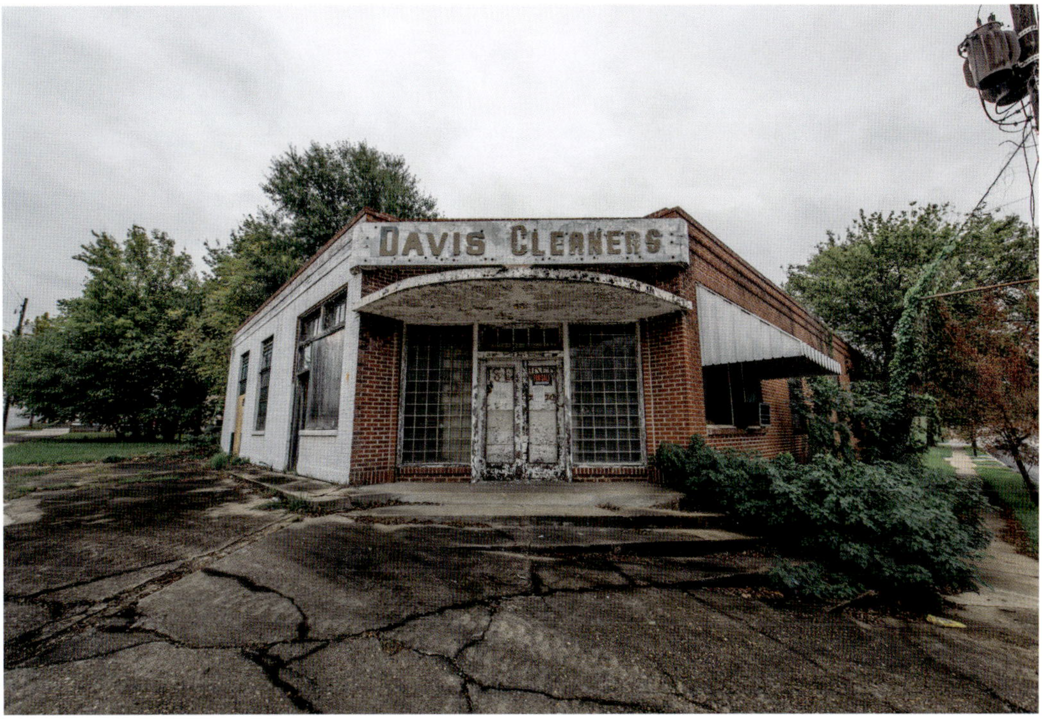

The smaller Empire-Rouse Laundry was dwarfed by the neighboring Capital City Cleaners in sheer size alone, let alone number of business locations.

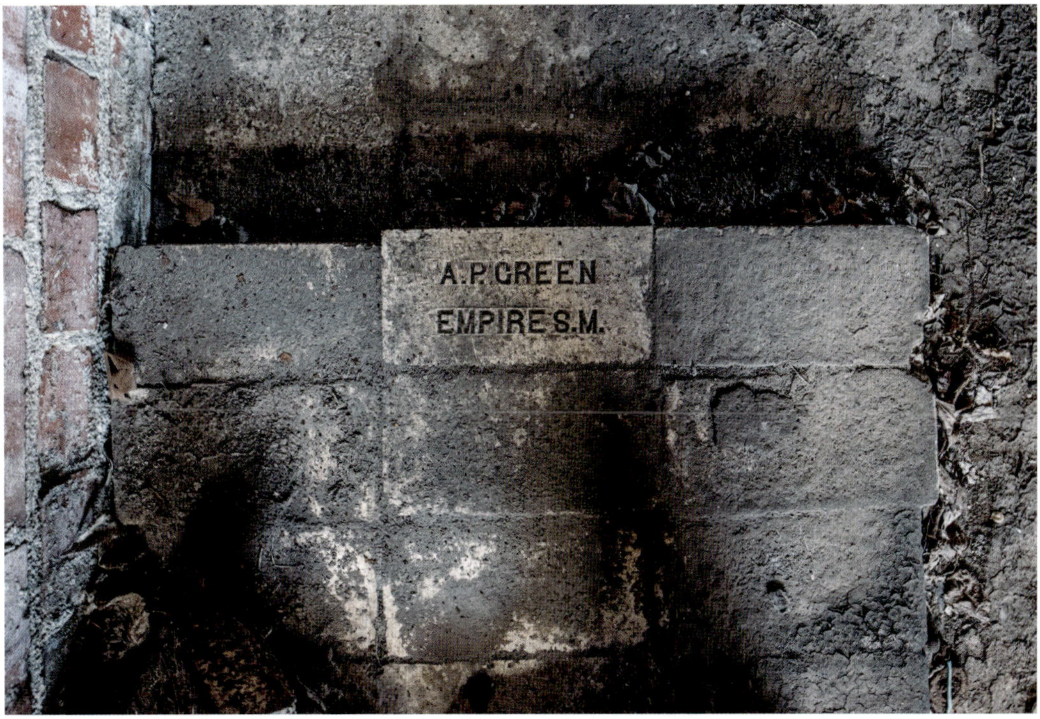

A lone brick with the inscription, "A. P. Green Empire S. M." In my research, I could not find what the initial meant.

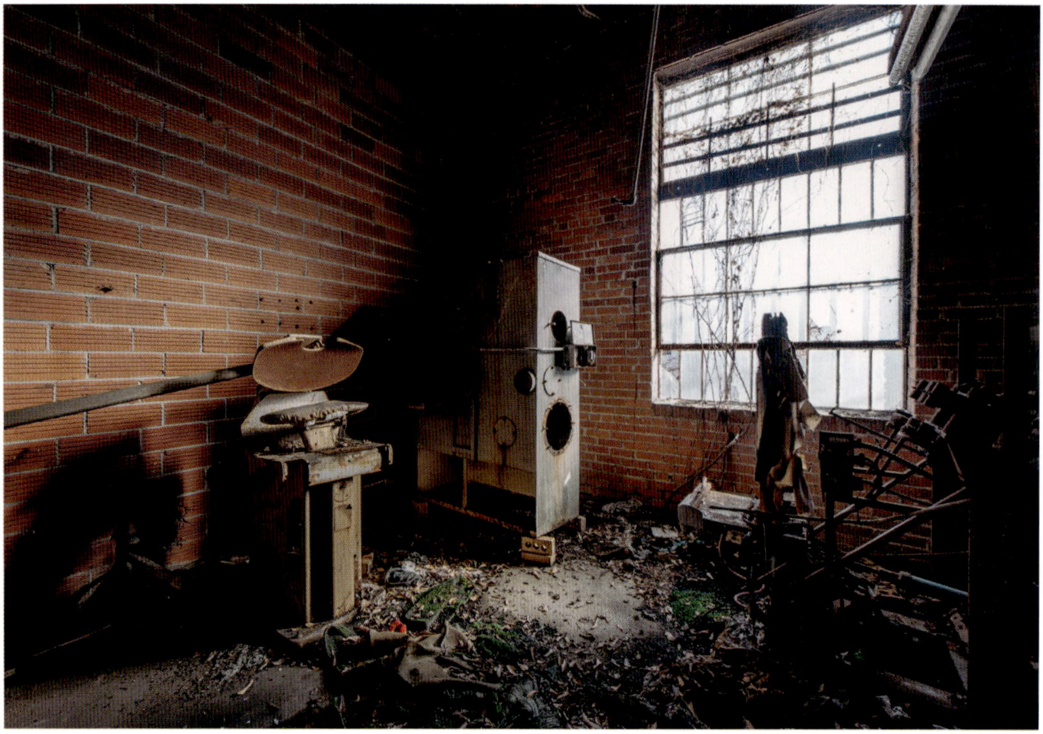

Here's a much smaller steam press than those found next door at the old Capital City Cleaners.

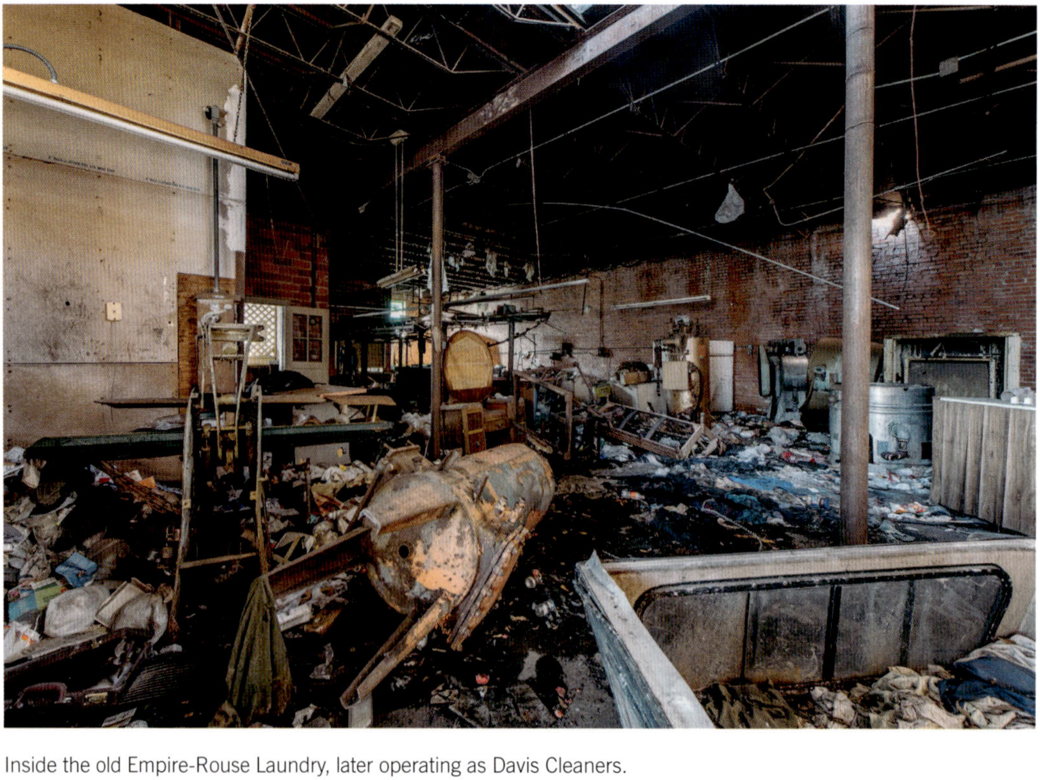

Inside the old Empire-Rouse Laundry, later operating as Davis Cleaners.

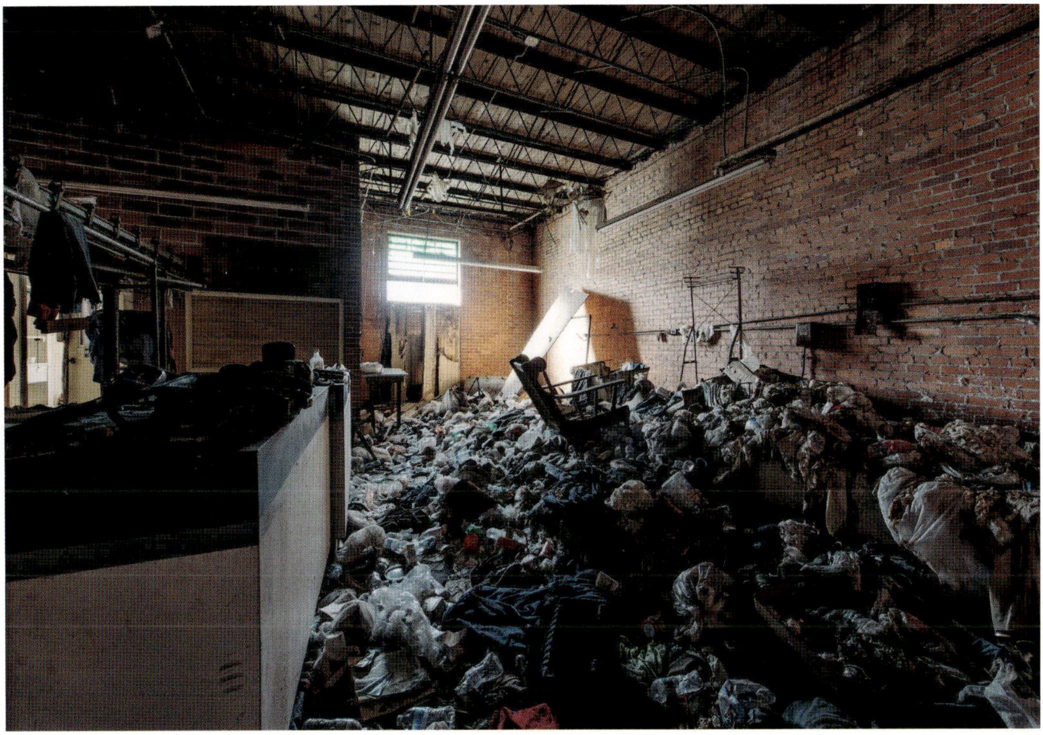

Piles upon piles of garbage and human waste.

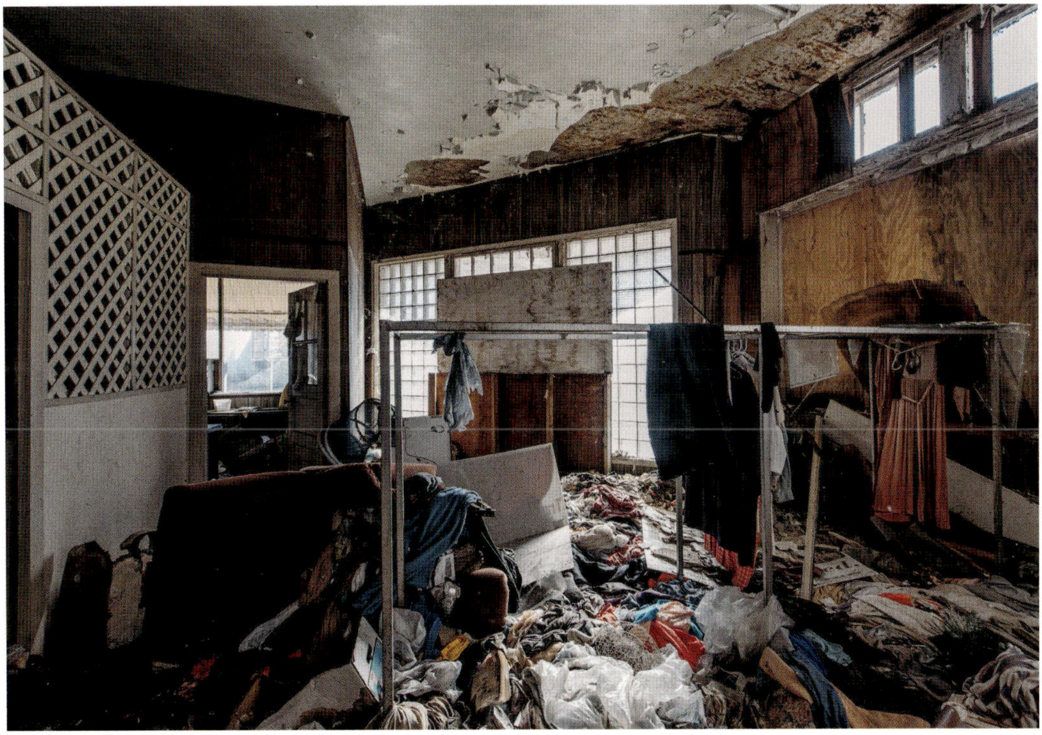

The front entrance of the former Empire-Rouse business.

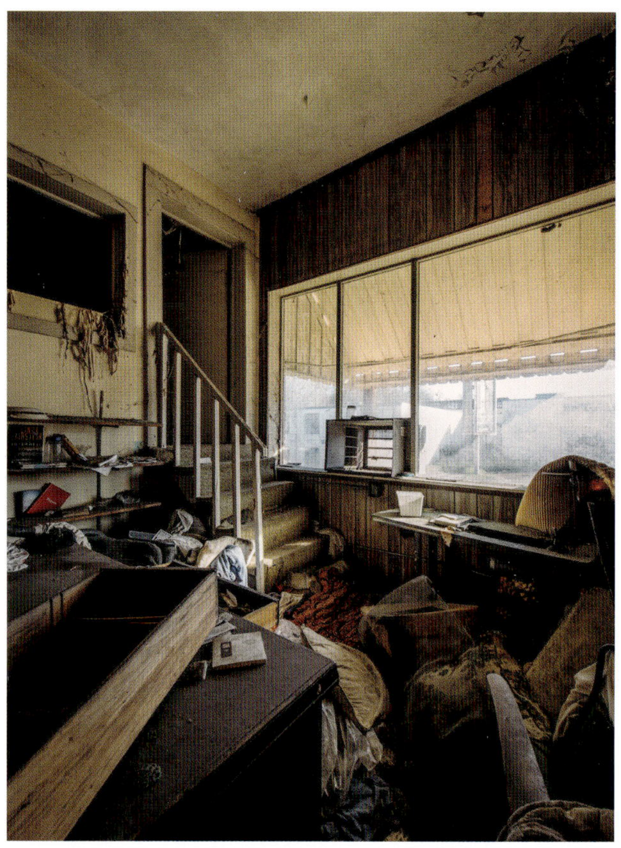

Left: Inside the small management office.

Below: An industrial sized wringer located down in the basement of the building.

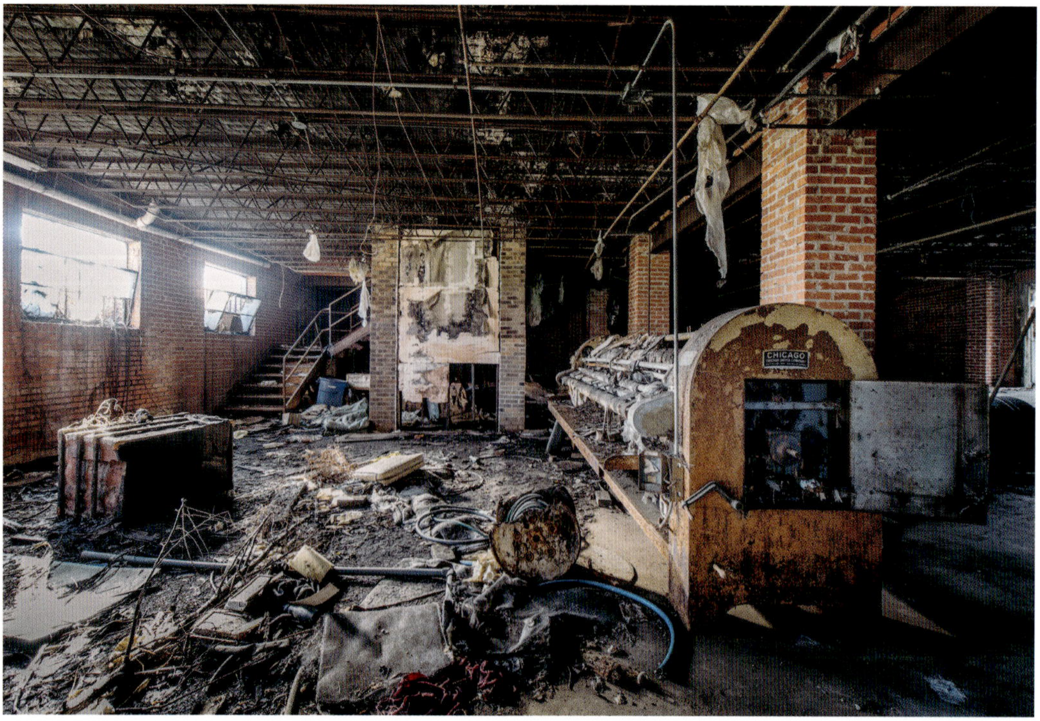

6

ST. JOHN THE BAPTIST CATHOLIC CHURCH

Built in 1913, St. John the Baptist Catholic Church is located in Montgomery in the historic Centennial Hill neighborhood. The church was one of many built within the neighborhood in the early part of the twentieth century. Centennial Hill grew around the historic First Congregational Church, which was established by the American Missionary Association (AMA) on October 6, 1872, by Pastor George Whitfield Andrews. In 1867, the AMA and the Freedmen's Bureau, headed by General Wager Swayne, opened Swayne Primary School, Montgomery's first school for black children. The Lincoln School of Marion was established that same year by nine ex-slaves and taken over by the AMA in 1868. After a large fire destroyed most of the campus, the university was relocated to Montgomery where it eventually became Alabama State University.

The area gained prominence as the civic, religious, educational, business, and residential center for black notables such as businessman Victor Hugo Tulane who constructed the Victorian-style "Tulane Building" corner grocery store just northeast of St. John the Baptist Catholic Church; Dr. Cornelius Dorsette, the city's first black physician and the first licensed black physician in Alabama; Nat King Cole, who was born and raised in Centennial Hill; Rufus "Tee Tot" Payne, a blues musician and Hank Williams' mentor, lived in the neighborhood; and Martin Luther King Jr., a minister and leader of the civil rights movement, who lived at 309 S. Jackson Street.

While the actual church is still functioning, the building next door, which was likely the rectory, has sat vacant for decades with the interior gutted down to the wooden studs.

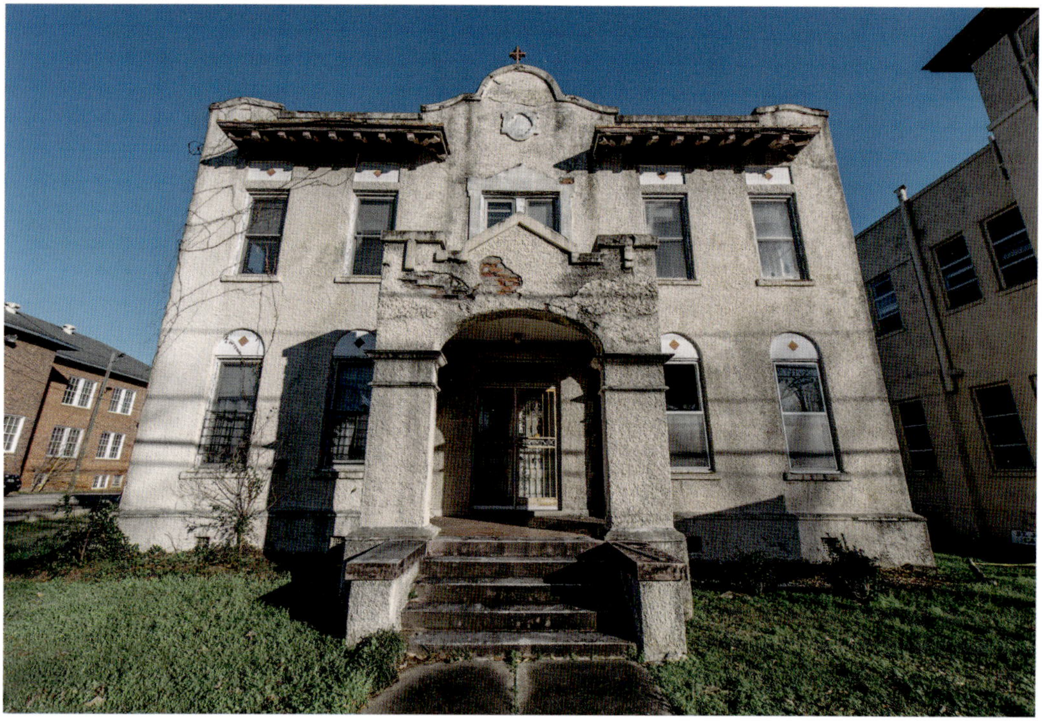

The church was designed to look like an adobe church seen throughout the Southwest United States, Central America, and parts of South America.

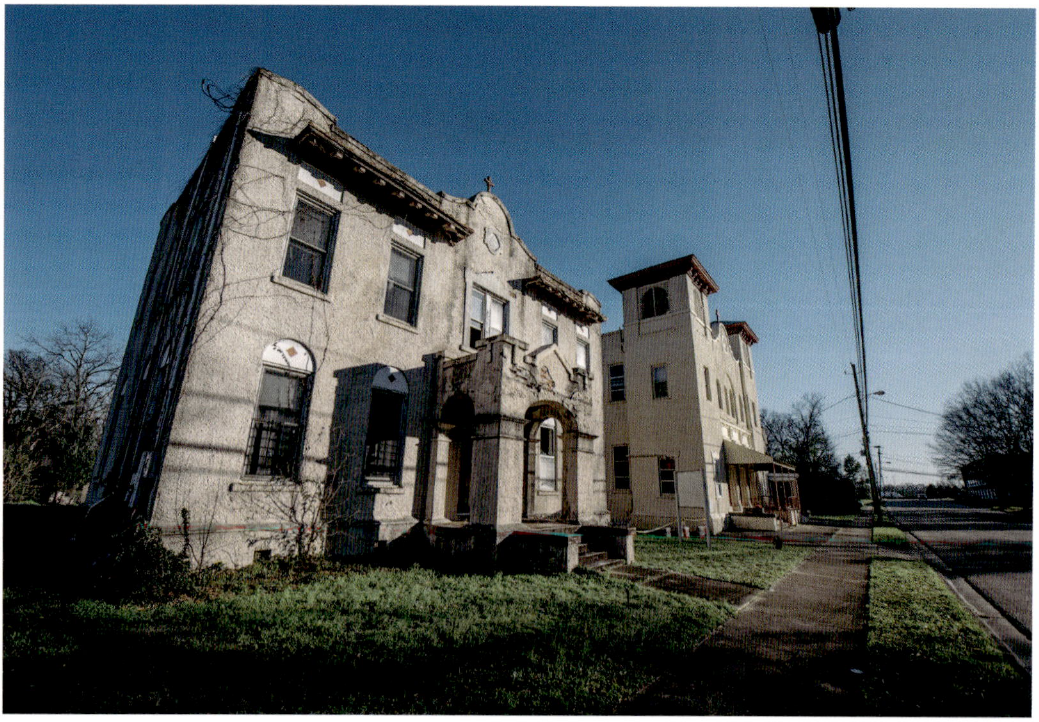

The actual church building remains active, but the building to the left has been abandoned for decades.

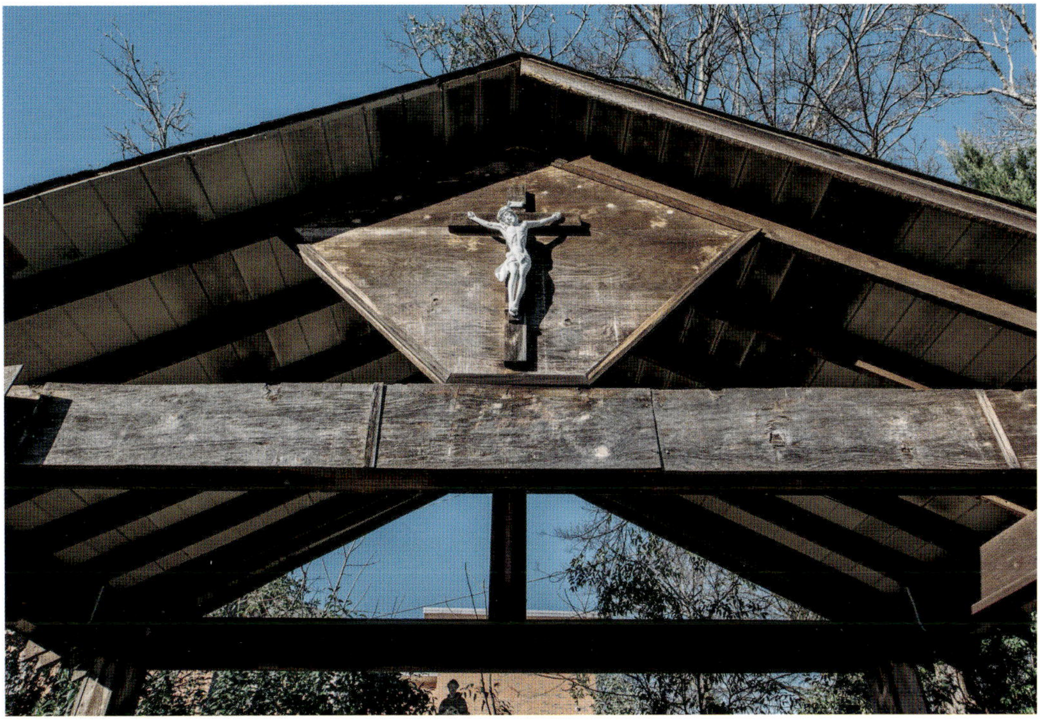

A small statue of Jesus Christ being crucified on the cross hangs above a gazebo behind the building.

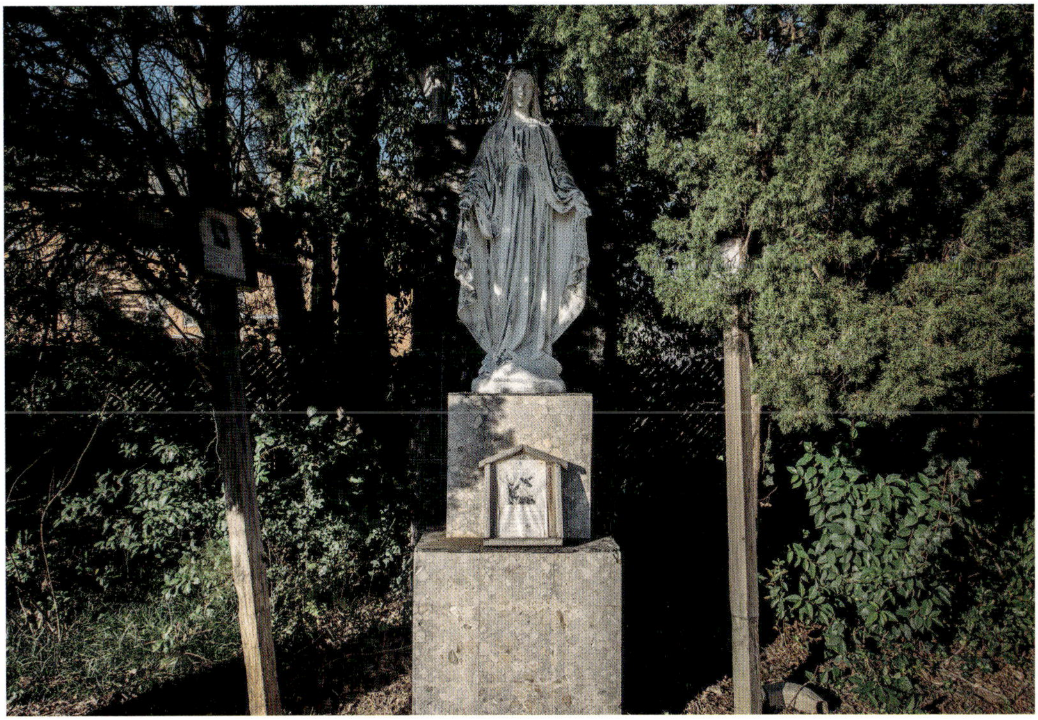

A statue of the Virgin Mary, damaged due to age and weather.

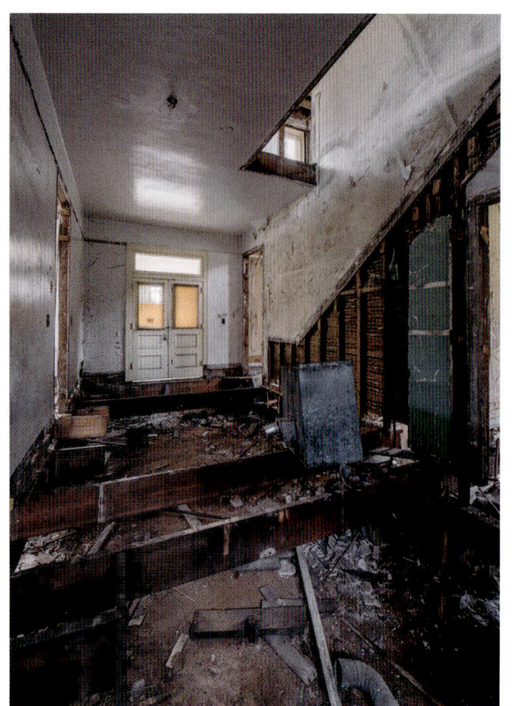

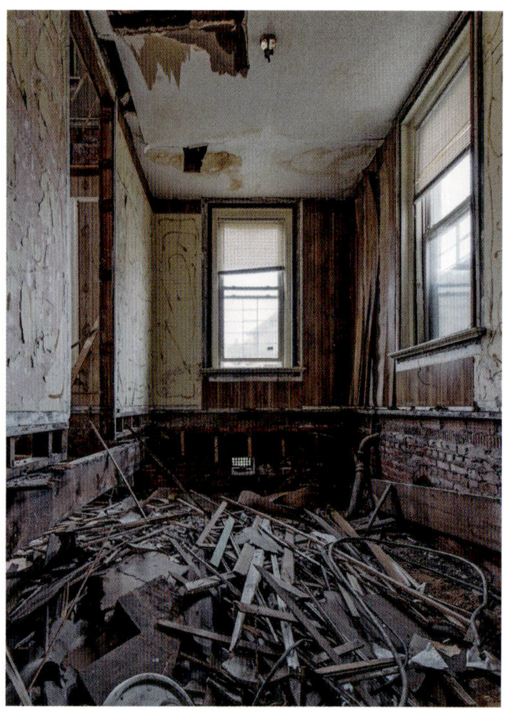

Above left: The interior staircase has been removed, making access to the second floor of the building not possible.

Above right: The floor is missing throughout the entire building.

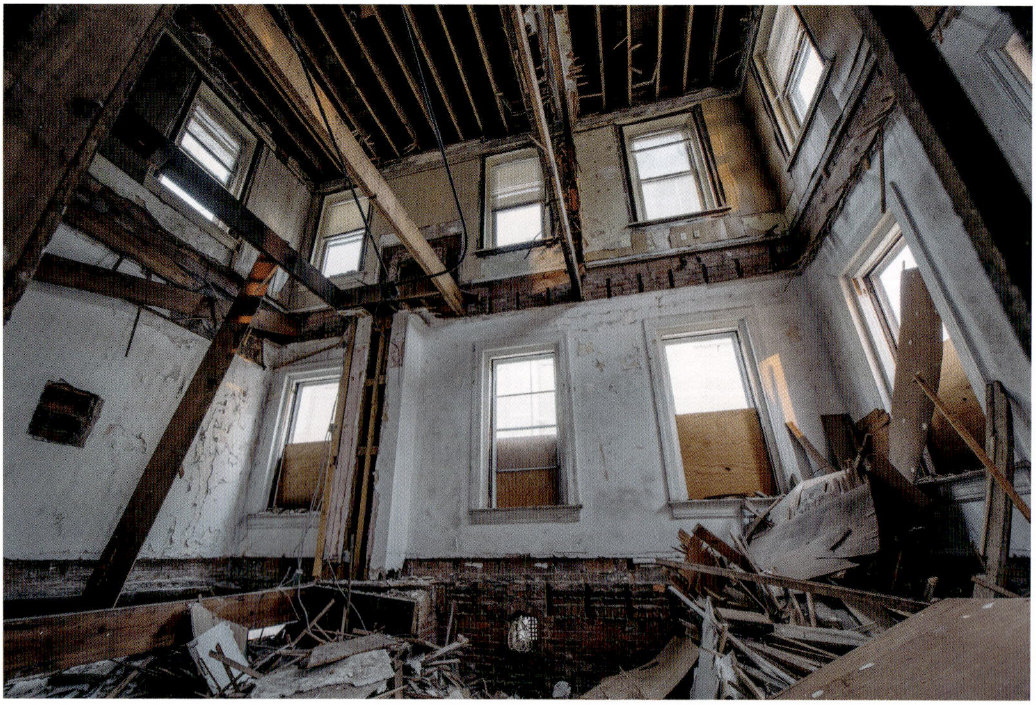

The interior looks to have been purposely gutted, possibly for a renovation that never happened.

7

GROVE COURT APARTMENTS

The Grove Court Apartments were built in 1947 by Bear Brothers construction company, owned by Carl W. Bear and his brothers, Joe and Jack Bear. The company was looking to fill part of the influx of population due to soldiers coming back from the war.

Consisting of three three-story reinforced concrete International Style apartment buildings, the complex was designed by Clyde C. Pearson and Farrow L. Tittle architectural firm with Parker A. Narrows and John H. Hancock associates. Clyde Collins Pearson was a 1926 graduate of the Alabama Polytechnic Institute (now Auburn University) and worked as a draftsman between 1925 and 1928, first with Frederick Ansfeld, then with Harry Wheelock, and finally with Warren, Knight, and Davis in Birmingham. He served as the architect for the Alabama State Department of Education between 1928 and 1933 and again from 1935 to 1941. Around this time, Pearson was also an architect for the National Park Service. He established his own architecture firm in Montgomery in 1941 and served as the president of the Alabama Council of the American Institute of Architects in 1942 and 1943.

The Grove Court Apartments earned recognition in the field of design, being awarded a "Mention" in the Progressive Architecture Awards of 1947 and featured in the June 1948 and February 1949 issues of *Progressive Architecture Magazine*. The apartments also won an American Institute of Architects Award.

The Grove Court Apartments is the only example of an International Style apartment complex in the city of Montgomery and is just one of a few remaining International Style buildings left in the city. The complex was recognized for its architectural value and was added to Places in Peril in 2009 by the Alabama Historical Commission and the Alabama Trust for Historic Preservation. In 2013, it was added to the National Register of Historic Places.

Since the 1980s, the complex had been in a state of decline, but operated through the 1990s and has been shut down for decades. Nearby businesses have complained throughout the years about the trash and overgrowth around the building, leading to an increased amount of roaches, raccoons, and rats. The only people living here now are vagrants looking to take shelter for the evening.

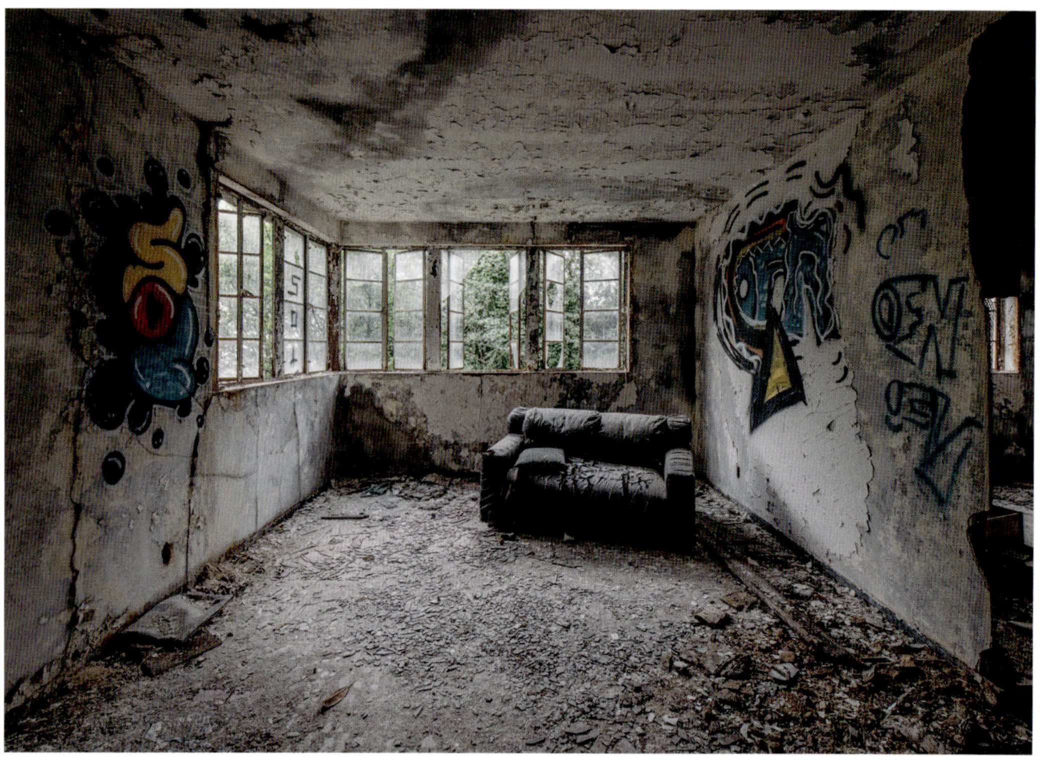

One can imagine how many homeless people have slept on this couch since the building's closure.

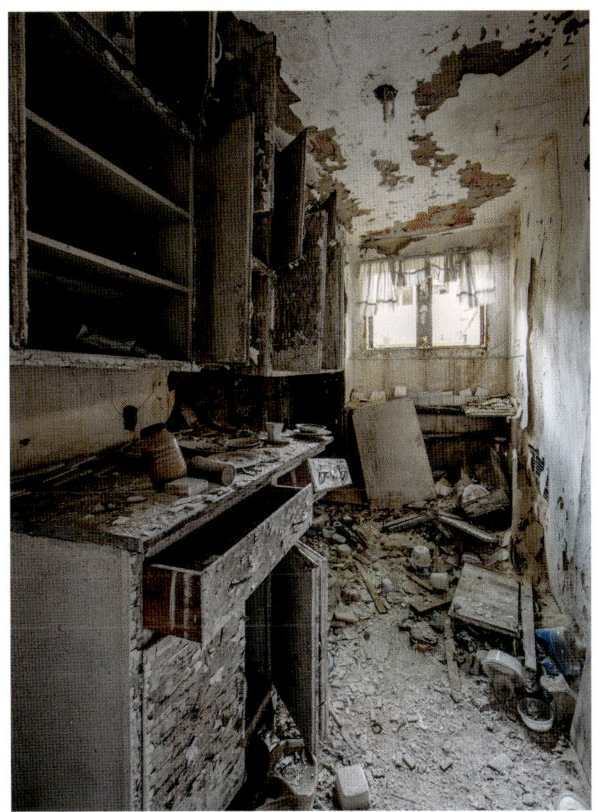

Right: The kitchen of one of the many apartments.

Below: One of the larger apartments, which comes with a balcony and an extra bedroom.

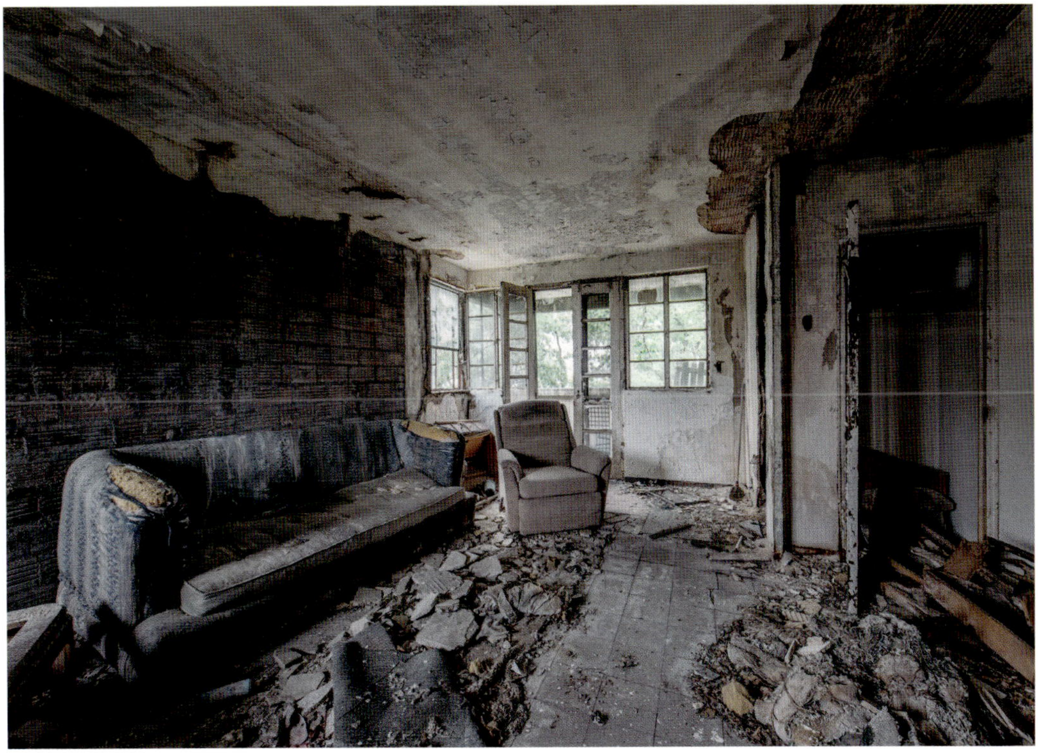

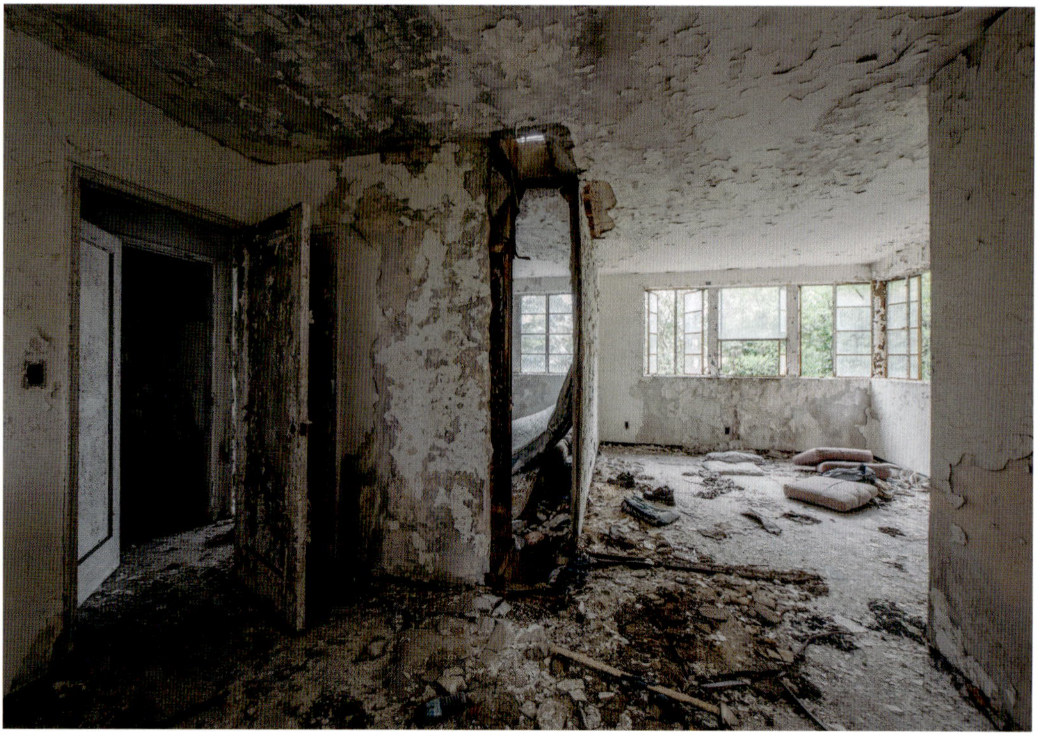

The hole in the middle once contained pipes for the bathroom, long removed by scrappers to be sold.

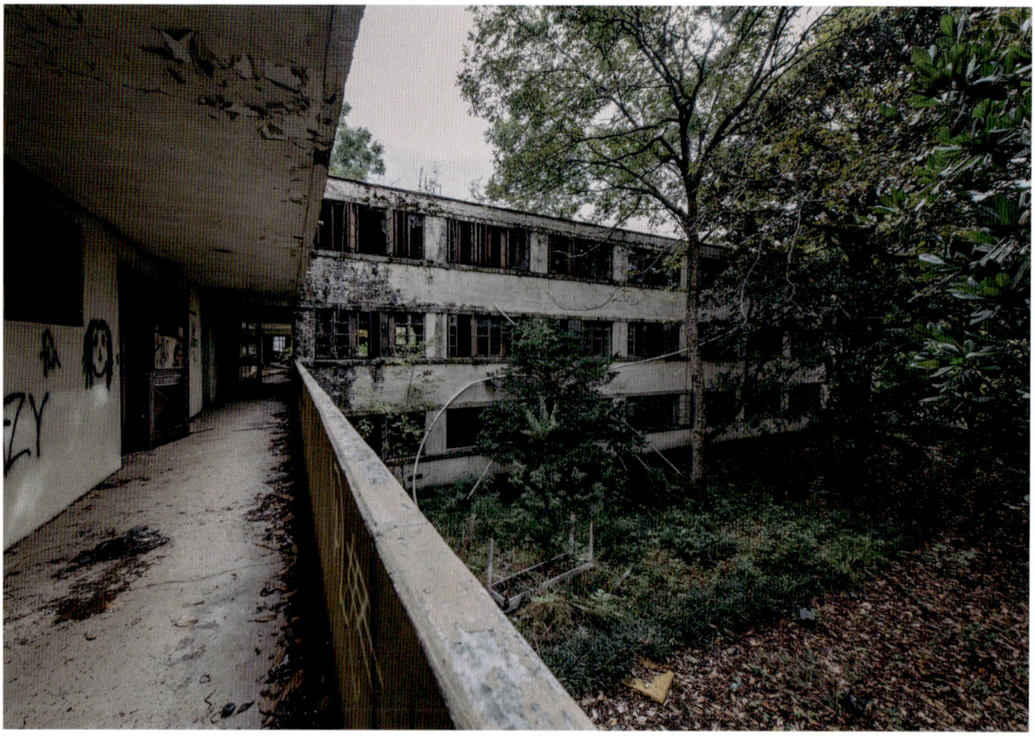

A view of the main courtyard from the second floor.

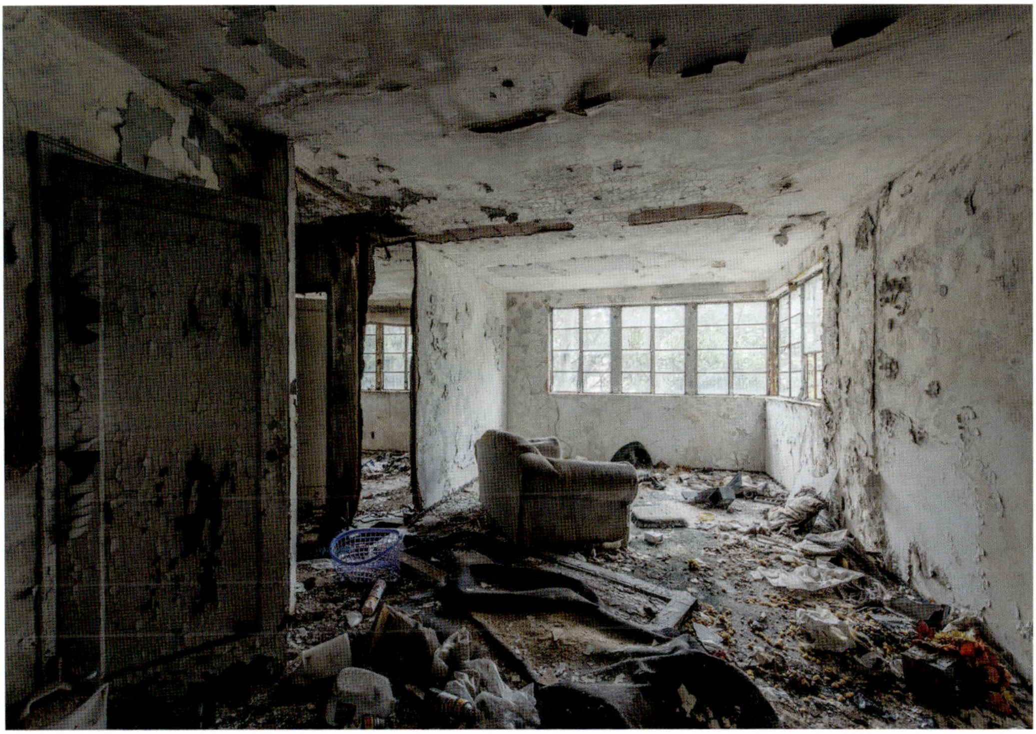

Trash and human waste litter this apartment, a sort of dumping ground for the homeless.

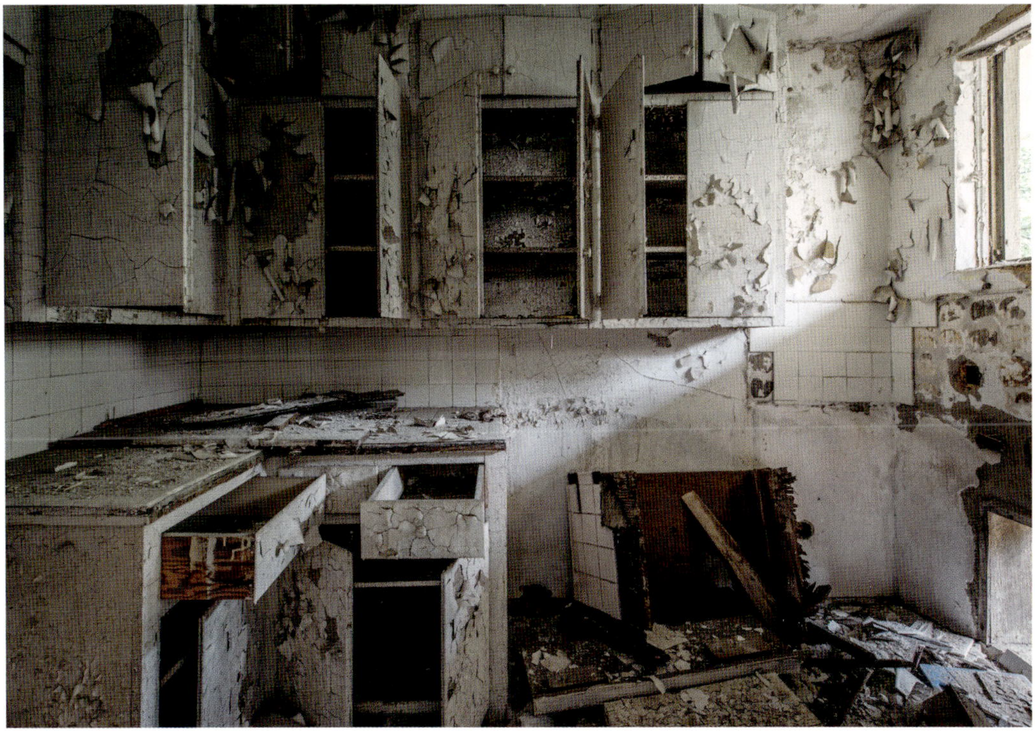

The kitchen sink has long been removed, along with its piping, to be sold.

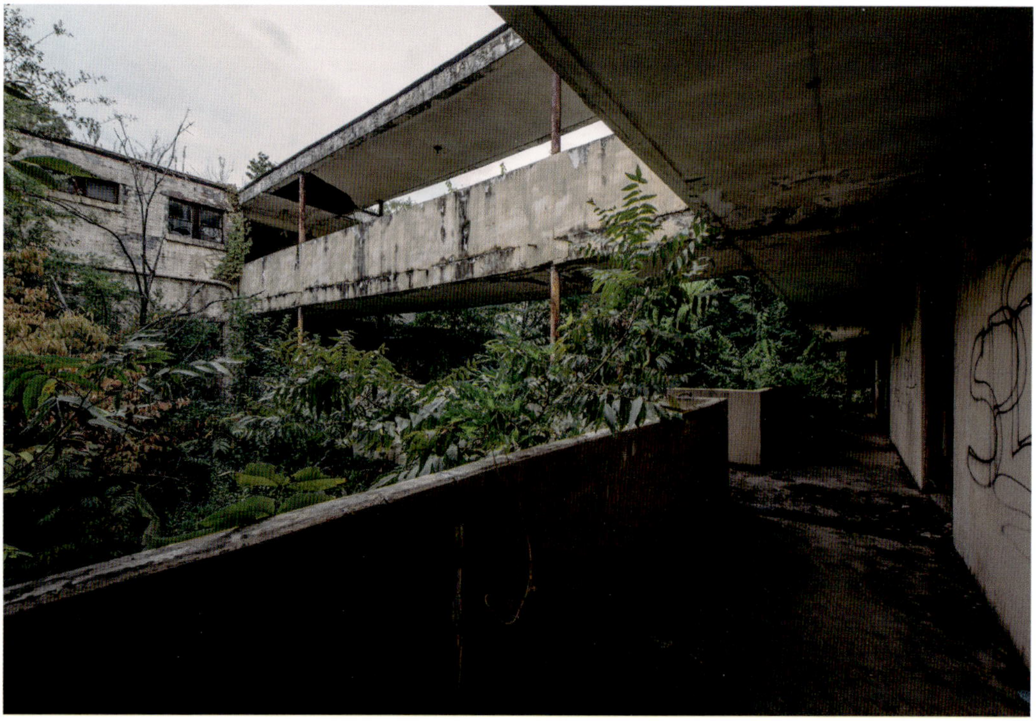

Due to lack of maintenance, the building's courtyards are overgrown.

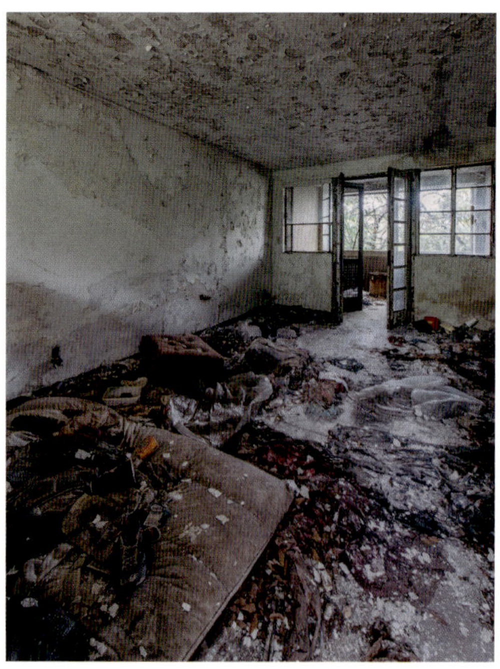

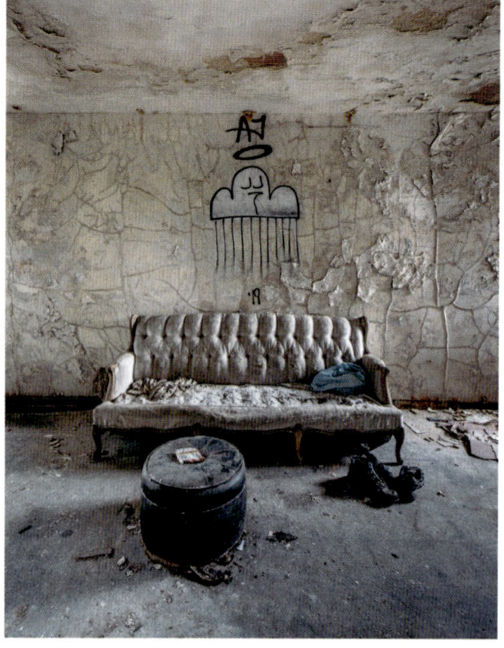

Above left: A mattress, shoes, and other signs that this room was used by a homeless individual as their camp for a while.

Above right: One of the nicer couches left in the building, a bed to those staying in the building for the night.

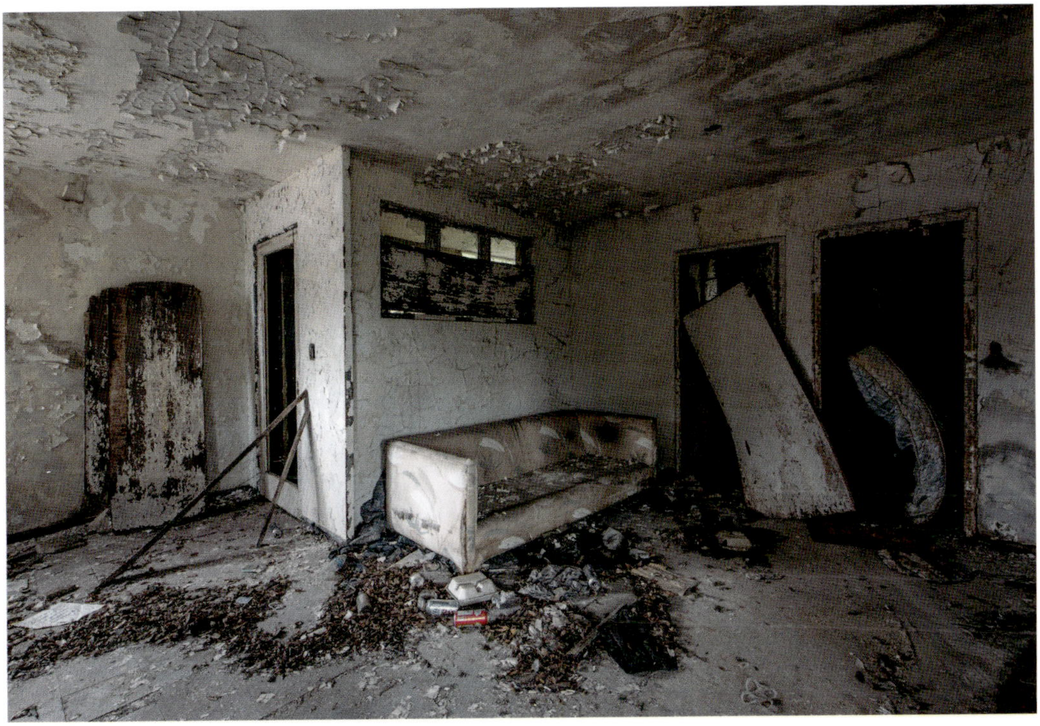

Empty beer cans and liquor bottles are a common sight at the Grove Court Apartments.

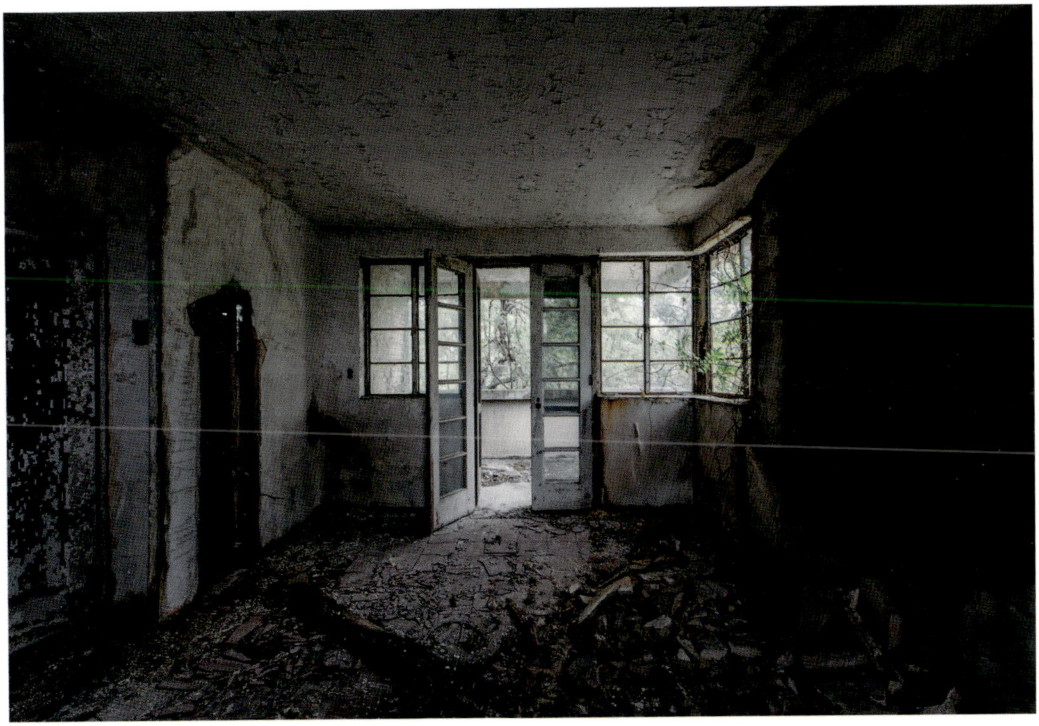

One can imagine how nice it must've been to open the balcony doors on a hot summer day.

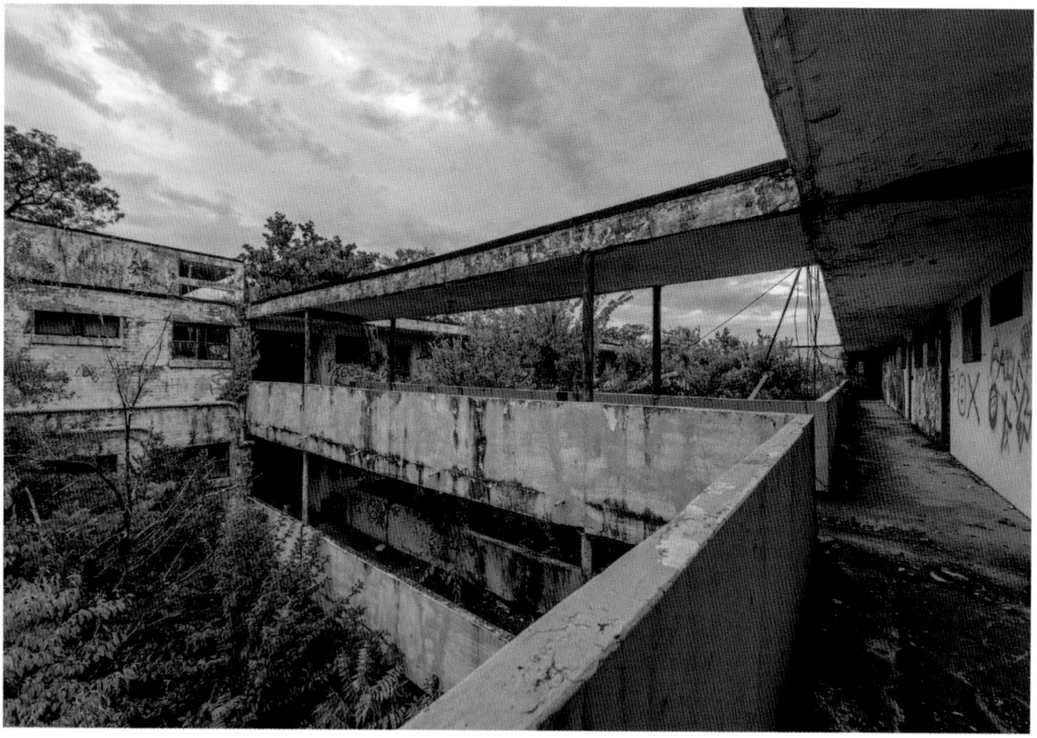

The overgrowth of the courtyards extends up to the top floor of the building.

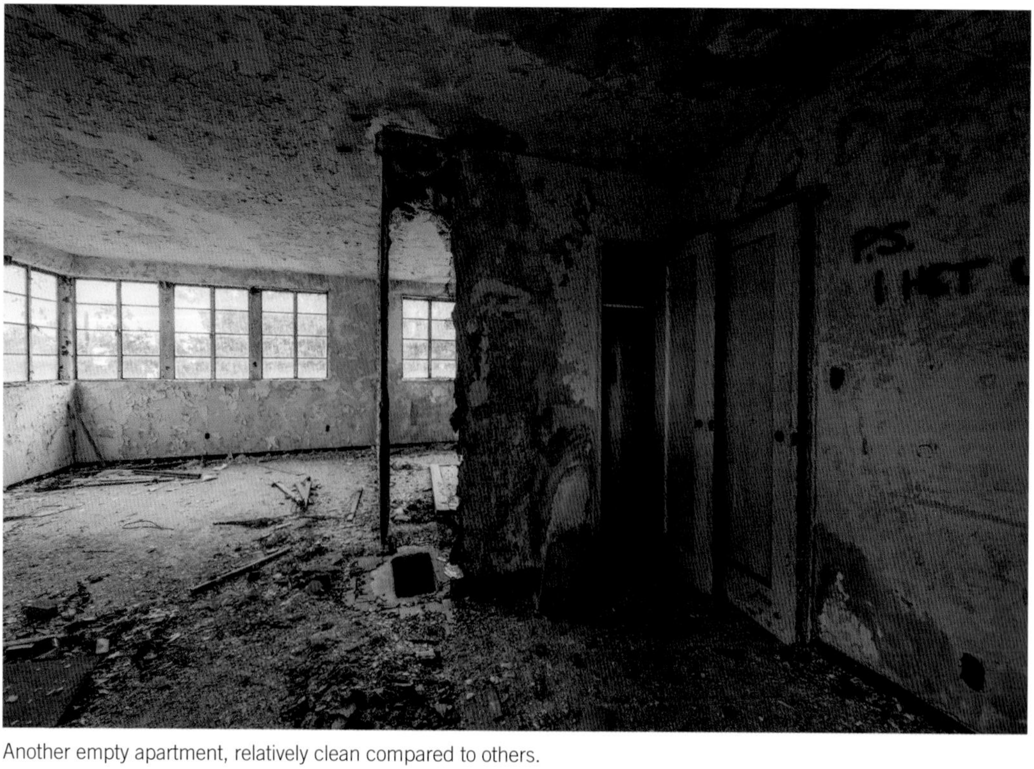

Another empty apartment, relatively clean compared to others.

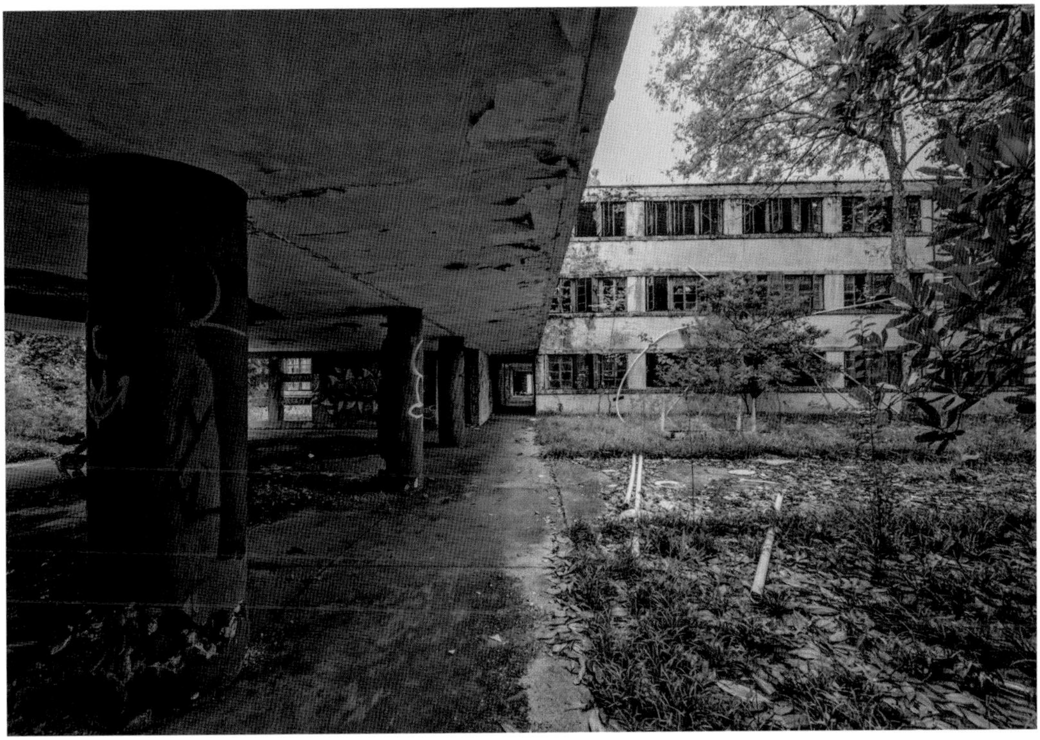

The ground floor near the front entrance to the Grove Court Apartments.

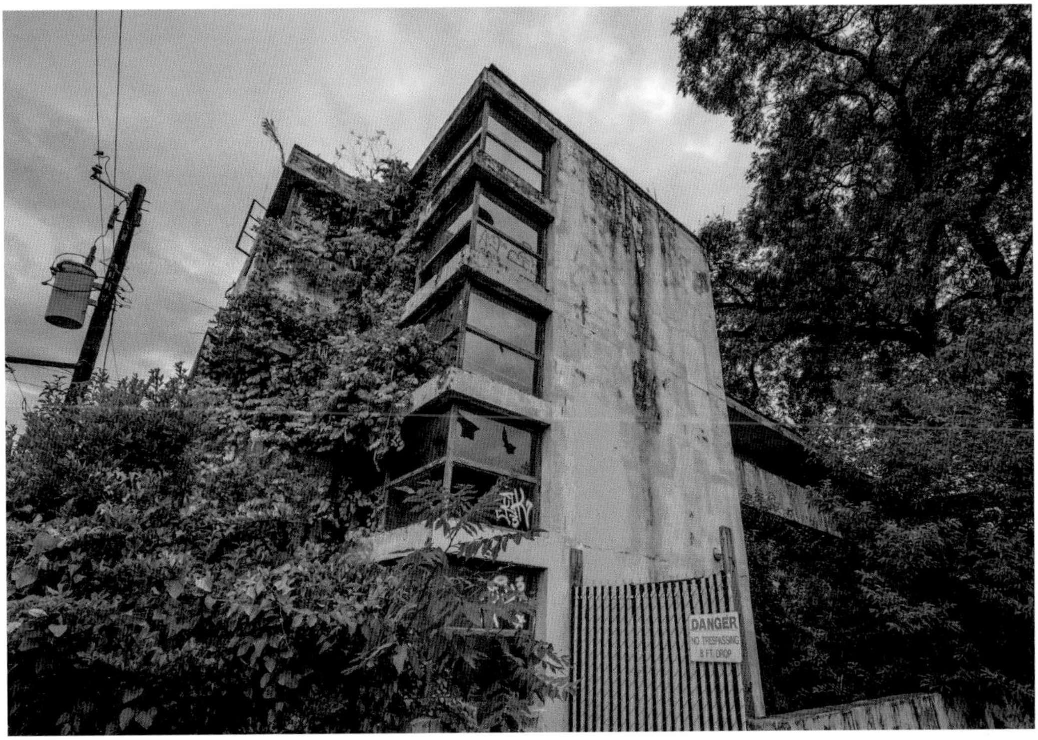

In the bottom right, a "No Trespassing" sign warns of a 6-foot drop just beyond the fencing.

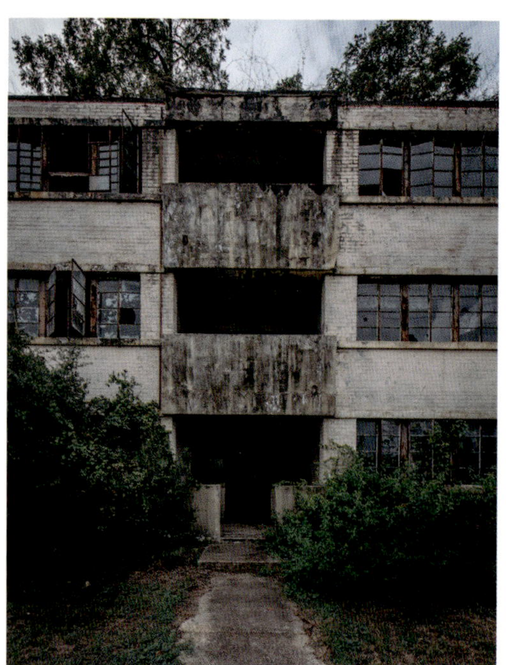

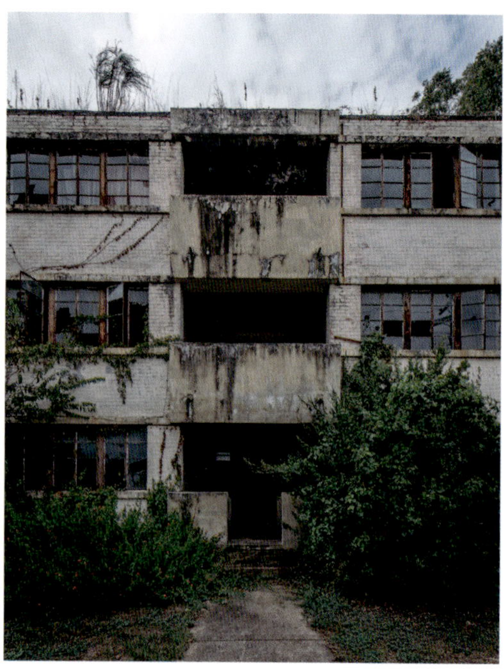

Above left: A view of one of the side entrances into one of the higher-end apartments.

Above right: Just after I snapped this photo, a man appeared in the top right window and told to move on and stop taking pictures.

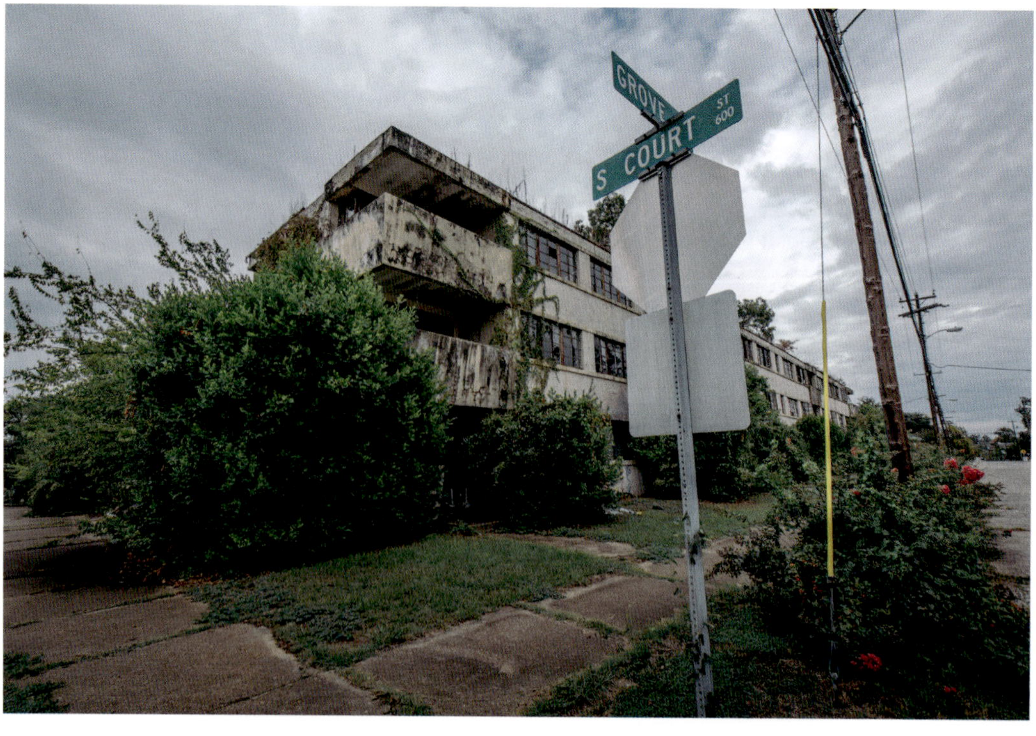

The Grove Court Apartments gets its name for the corner it sits on, Grove and Court Streets.

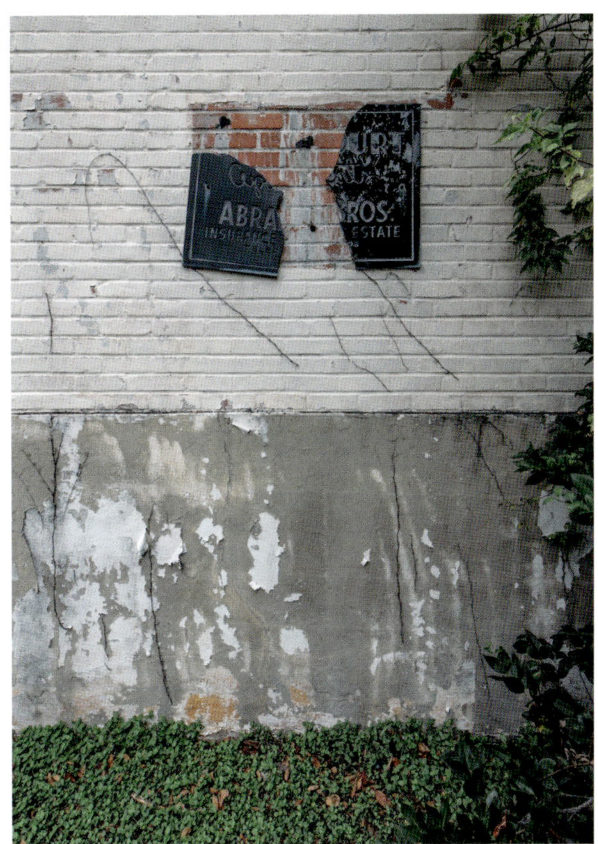

Above left: A broken sign which once read "Grove Court Apartments."

Above right: The front entrance to the building has long been boarded up, although there are still many ways into the building.

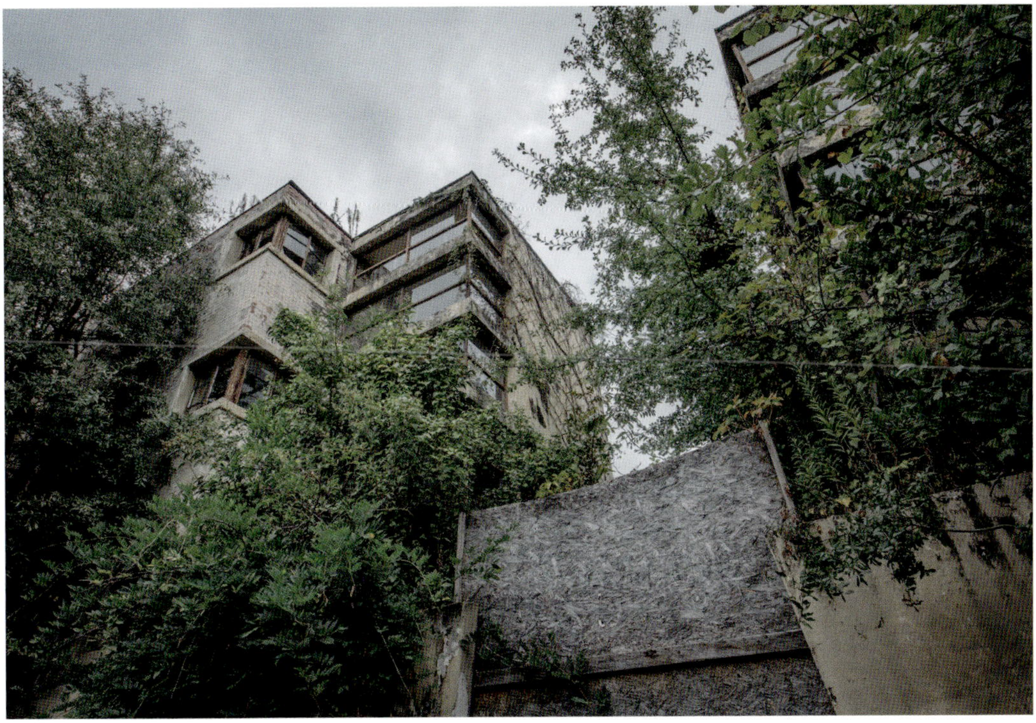

8

SAYRE STREET SCHOOL

The Sayre Street School is the oldest surviving public-school building in Montgomery. Its history dates back to before the Civil War when a private boys' school, the Franklin Academy, was located on the site. In 1863, the Franklin Academy was put up for sale and it can be assumed that it was purchased by Dr. Samuel K. Cox and renamed the Cox College. Dr. Cox was a Protestant Methodist minister of Montgomery, a president of a female college in Montgomery, and was associated with Mrs. Pollock, who was well-known for establishing the all-girls Pollock-Stephen Institute in Birmingham. Following the Civil War, Dr. Cox left Montgomery to Christiansburg, Virginia, to work at a college there.

Chilton College was a private school for girls and young women, established in Montgomery in 1866 by Mrs. Lavinia T. Bradford Chilton. The institution was named after William Parish Chilton of Tennessee, Zelda Sayre Fitzgerald's father-in-law and cousin to the Sayres. Chilton College was originally located on Felder Avenue before it was moved to the building formerly occupied by Cox College in 1972 and was renamed the Montgomery Female College.

The City Council, short on funds and unable to construct new buildings, began renting the property in the late 1870s for classrooms. With the improving economy of the 1880s, the city's School Committee was able to purchase the lot, building, and all shares related to the Montgomery Female College.

On June 24, 1885, the School Committee recommended that the upper floor chapel of the school building, now designated the Girls High School, be renovated by placing partitions to provide more classrooms. By this time, the City of Montgomery was renting out a wood-framed structure adjacent to the Girls High School and utilizing it as the Sayre Street Grammar School.

In 1888, the School Committee reported that all the rooms in the wood-framed structure needed repairs and that only three of the ten rooms were adequate enough to house the increasing number of students. At the end of the 1890 school year, the committee stated that the current buildings were "totally inadequate" and recommended the construction of a new building to replace the old ones. In 1891, Committee Chairman Alderman Watts presented a plan to the City Council for a new building and was granted approval for its construction.

Designed and built by J. B. Worthington, the new school building housed an elementary school on the first floor, and the Girls High School was located on the second floor. The old building had been marked by a marble slab inscribed "Chilton College." To commemorate its existence and also the educational work of Mrs. Chilton, the slab was placed at the base of the new Sayre Street School by Daughters of the American Revolution.

In 1899, the Girls High School was relocated to the site of the current Montgomery County main library. When Sidney Lanier High School was constructed in 1910 at the corner of McDonough Street and Scott Street, the city's Boys High School and Girls High School were both moved to this new school, forming Montgomery's first public co-educational school.

The Sayre Street School served grades one through six until 1976, when it closed due to a shift in the neighborhood's population and laws regarding integration from the Civil Rights Act. The building was sold to private investors and it served as office and event space for many years, hosting everything from birthday parties to funerals, until around 2017, when its last occupant left. The building was listed on the National Register of Historic Places in 1982.

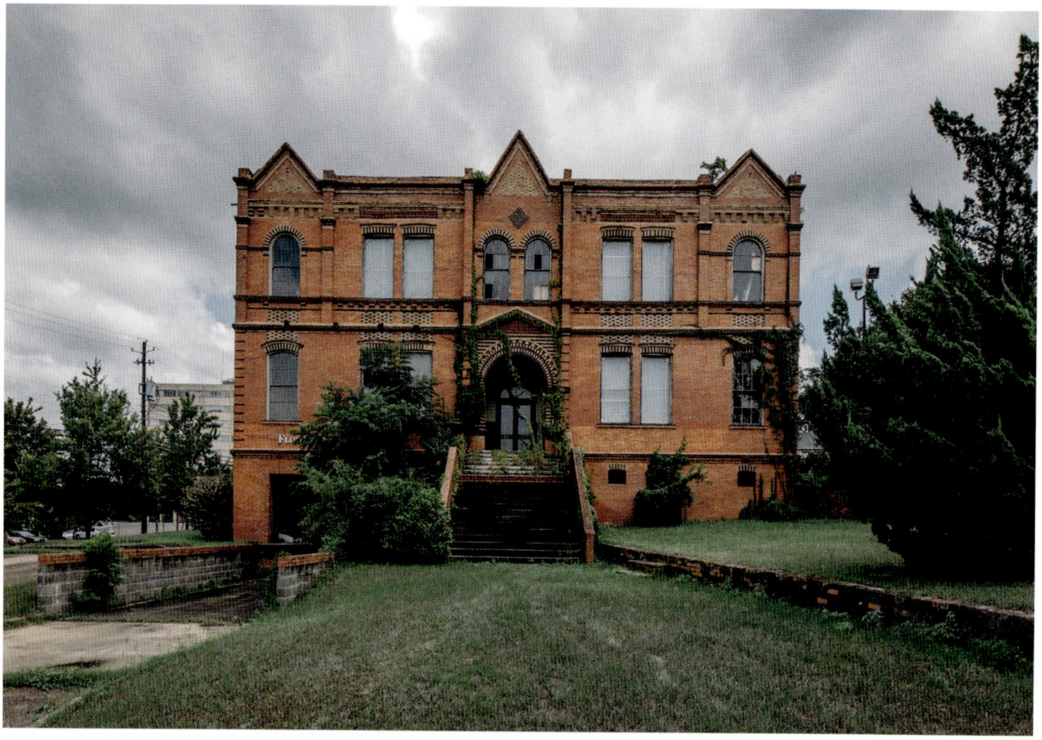

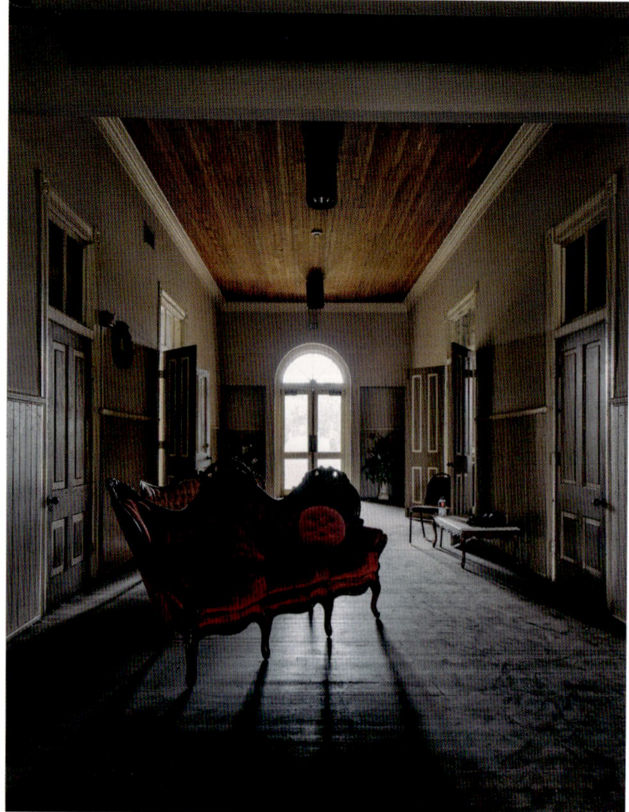

Above: The former schoolhouse has been also used as a funeral home, flower shop, and shared office space.

Left: Little hints of the modern age can be found throughout the building, such as the lights in the ceiling.

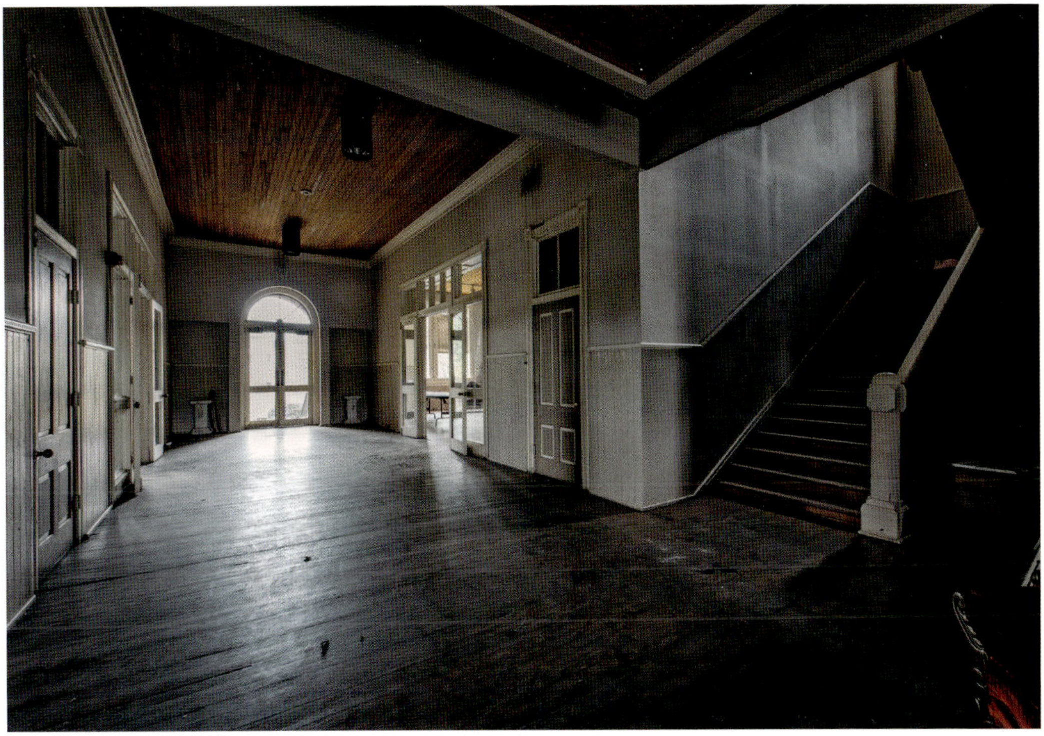

The main hall looking towards the front entrance.

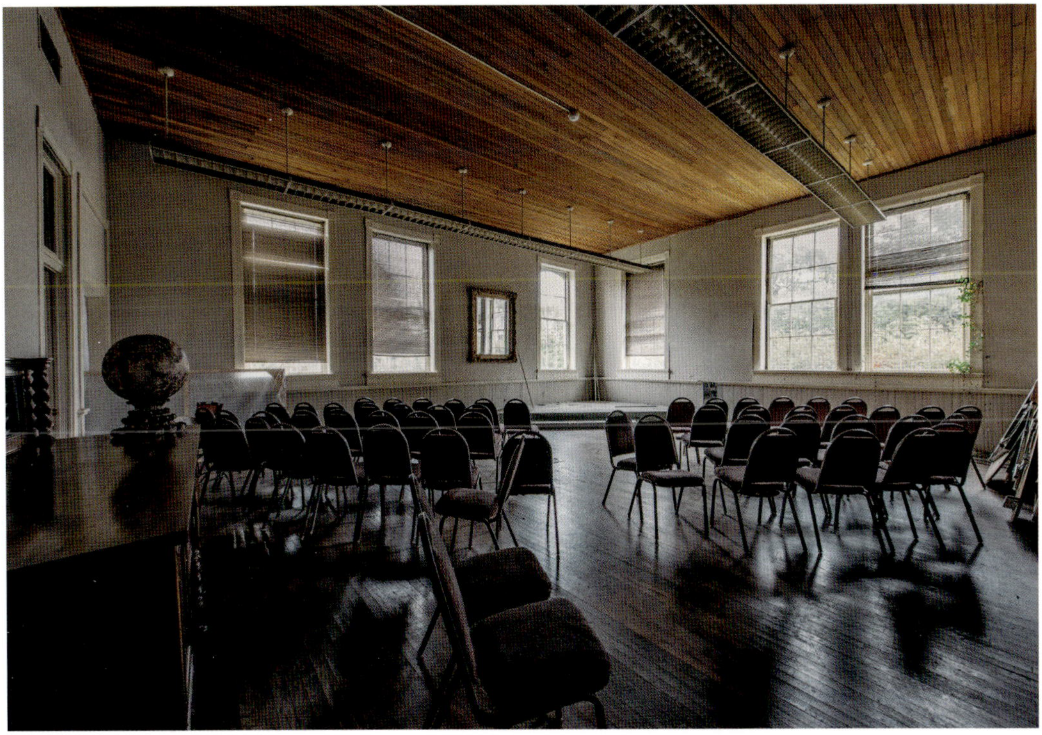

A gathering room used for events and for funeral wakes.

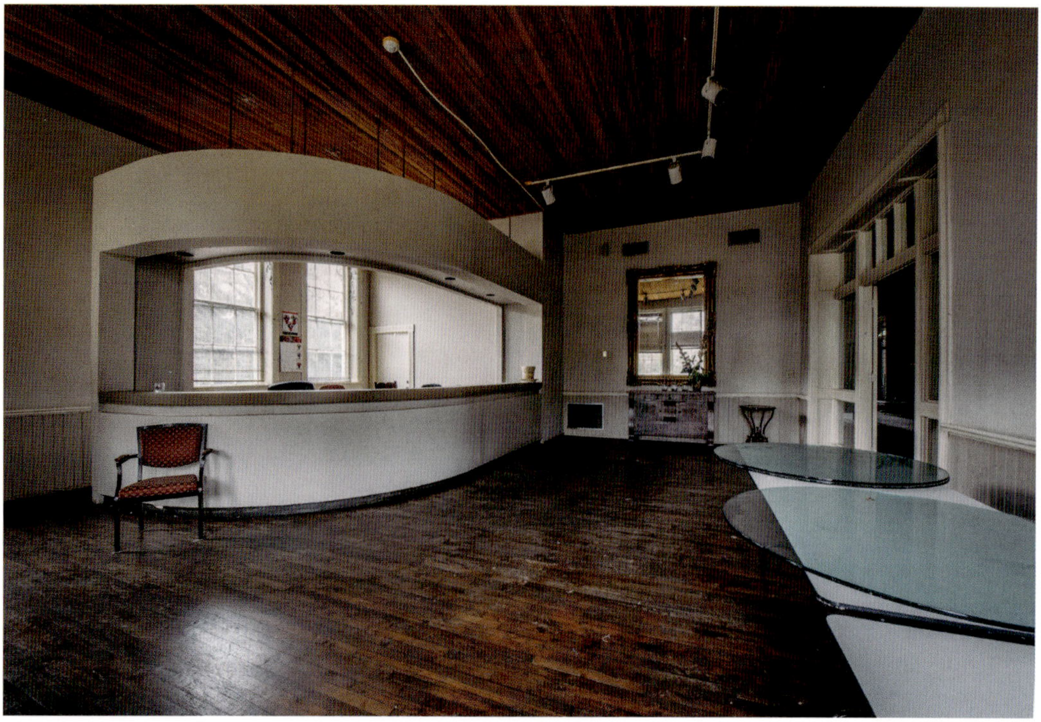

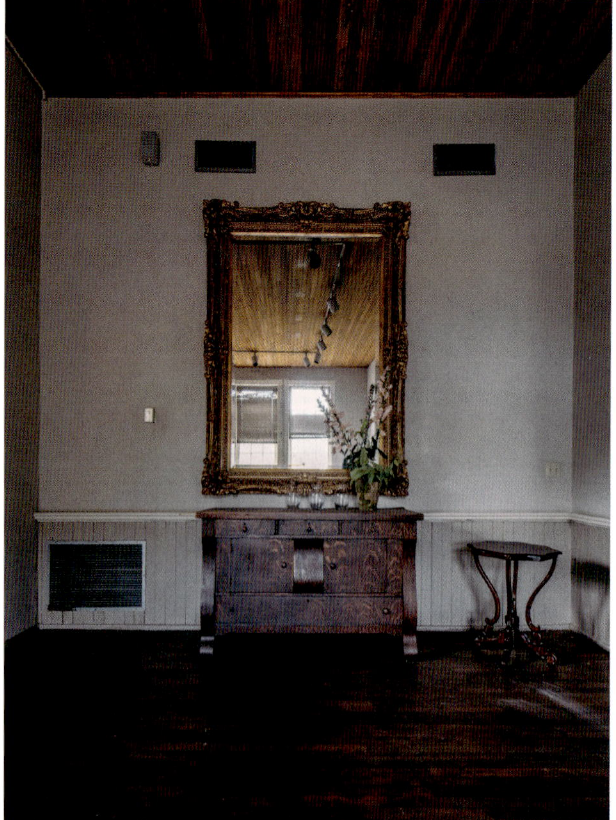

Above: A reception area in what most likely used to be a classroom.

Left: To get a sense as to how high the ceilings are, the mirror alone is probably 6-feet high.

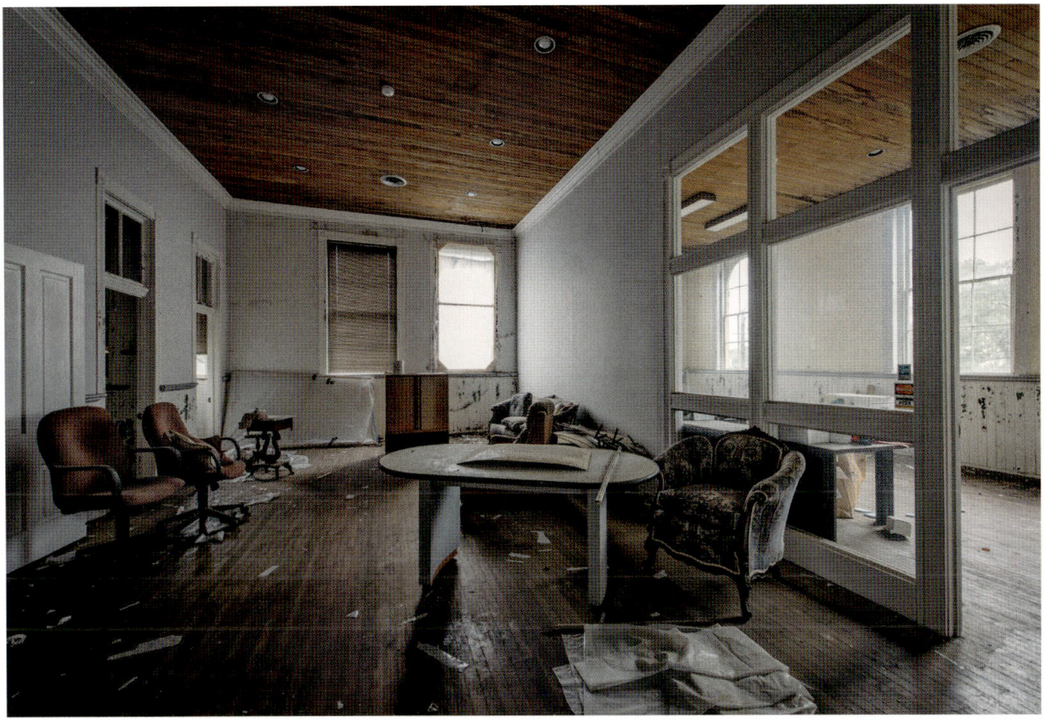

Blueprints remain on the table of the room for a planned renovation of the former schoolhouse that never came to be.

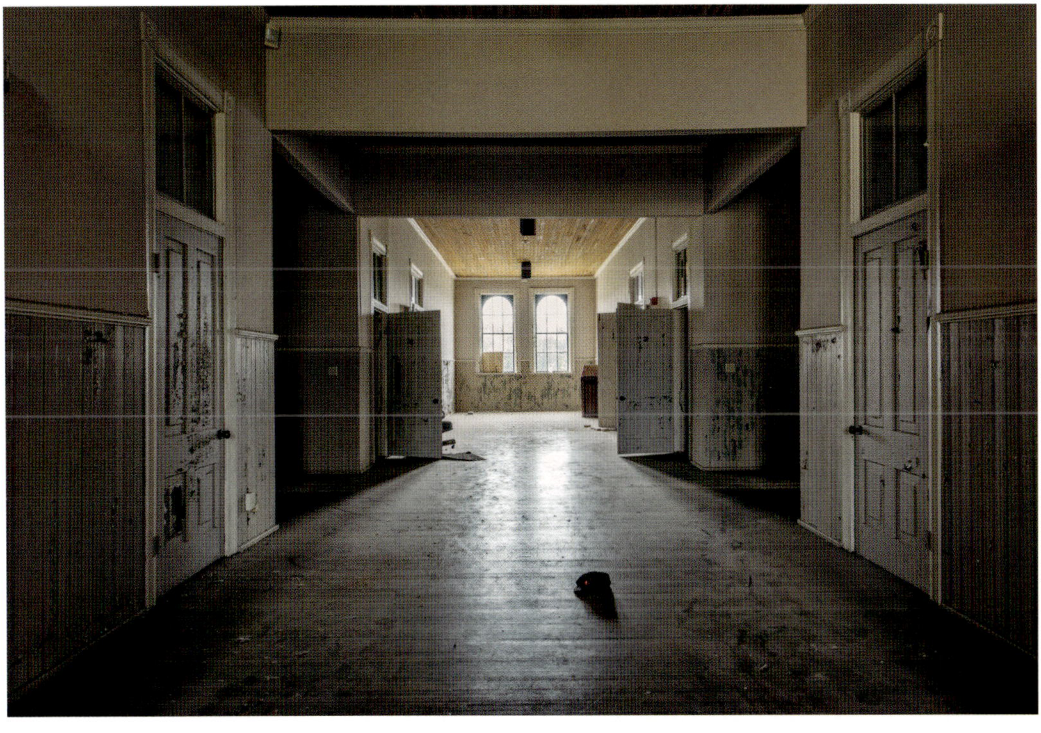

The second-floor hallway.

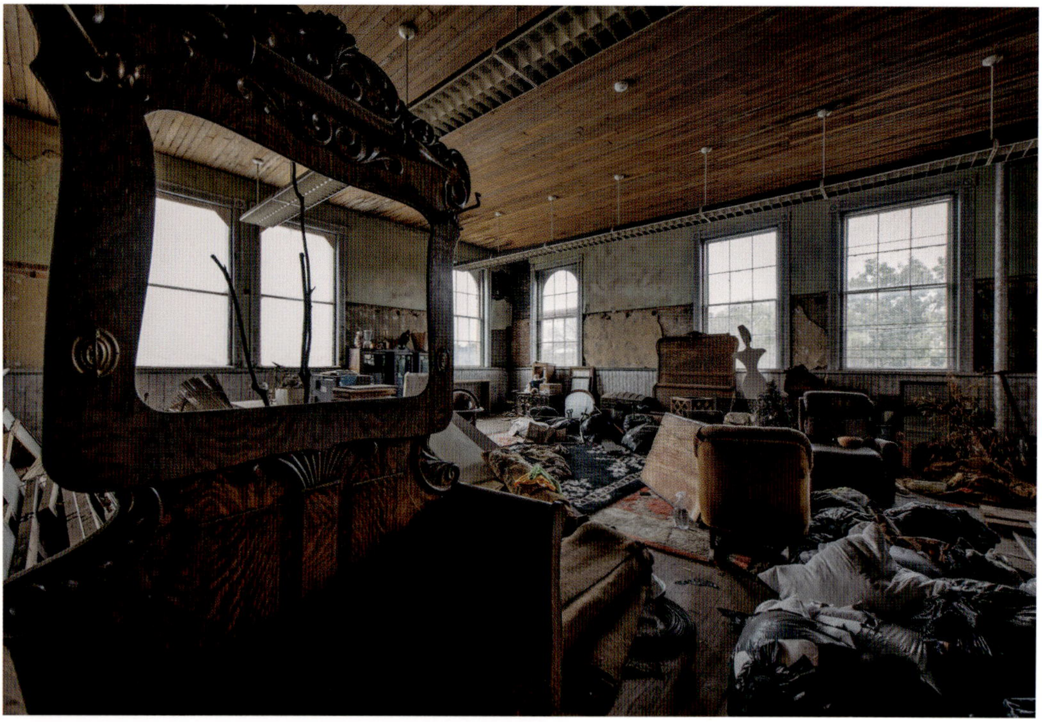

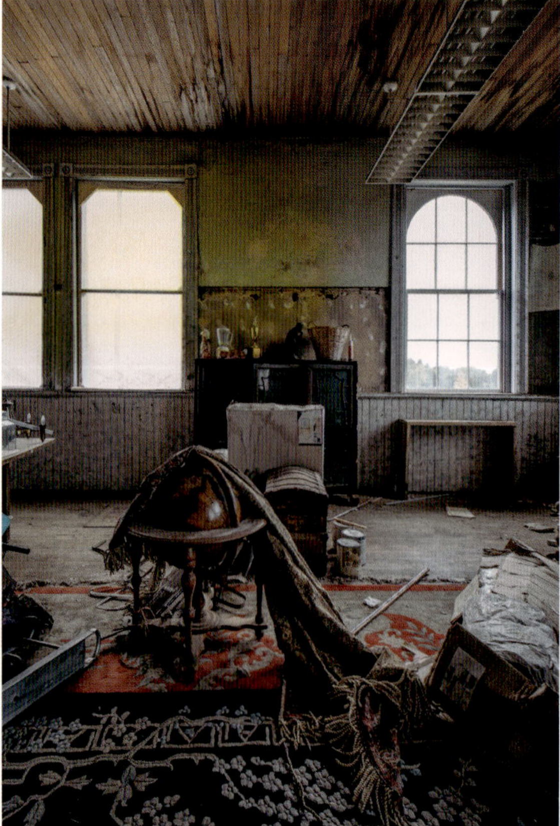

Above: Many of the former classrooms are packed with furniture, clothing, appliances, and construction equipment.

Left: A large globe is among the stuff packed into one of the former classrooms.

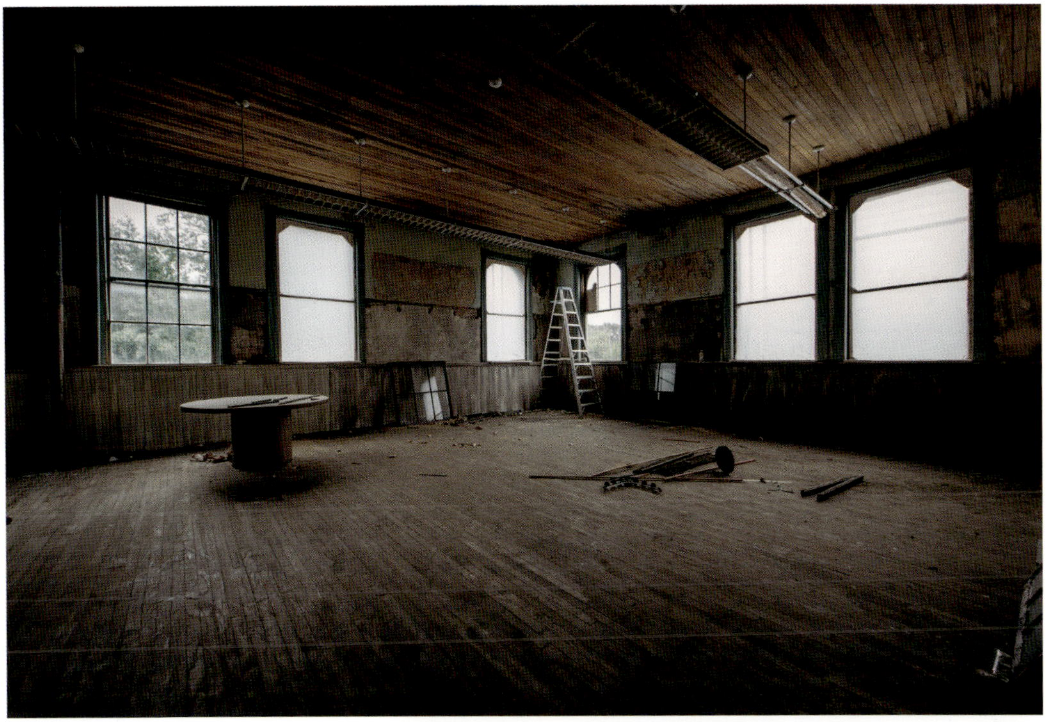

Above: One of the former classrooms with what looks like remnants of work stopped mid-renovation.

Right: The doorways alone are between 10-12 feet high.

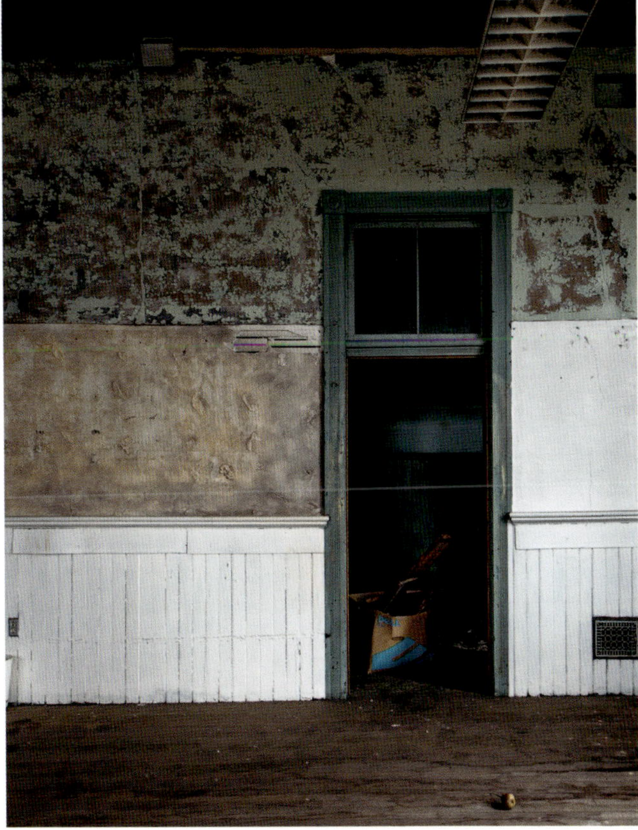

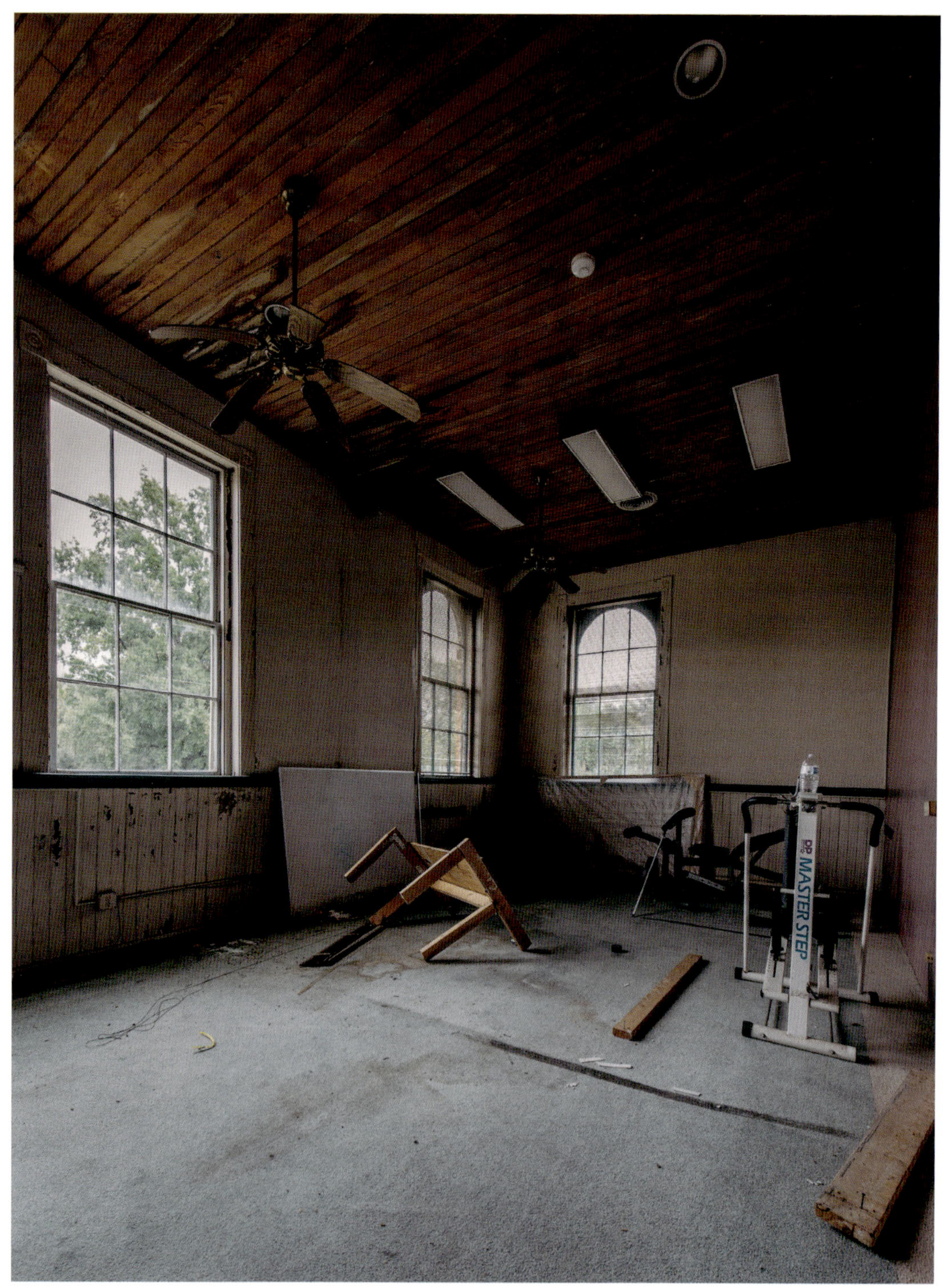

Water damage can be seen in the ceiling, a lot of work for whoever decides to buy the building.

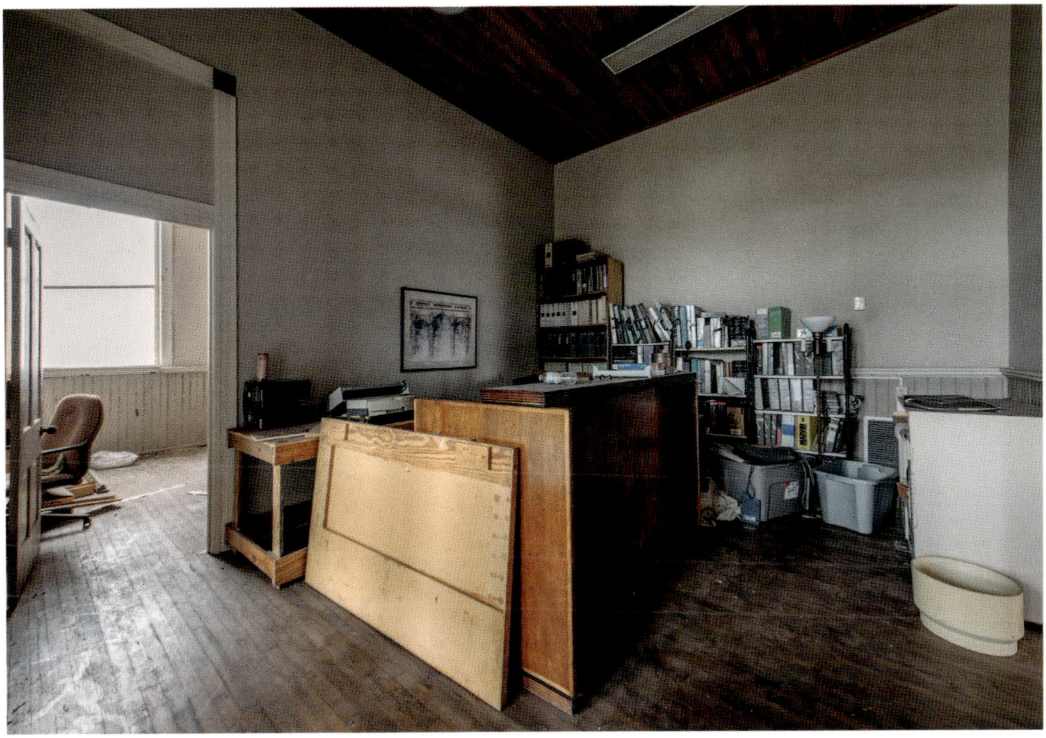

An office of some sort, probably used by when the building served as an office building.

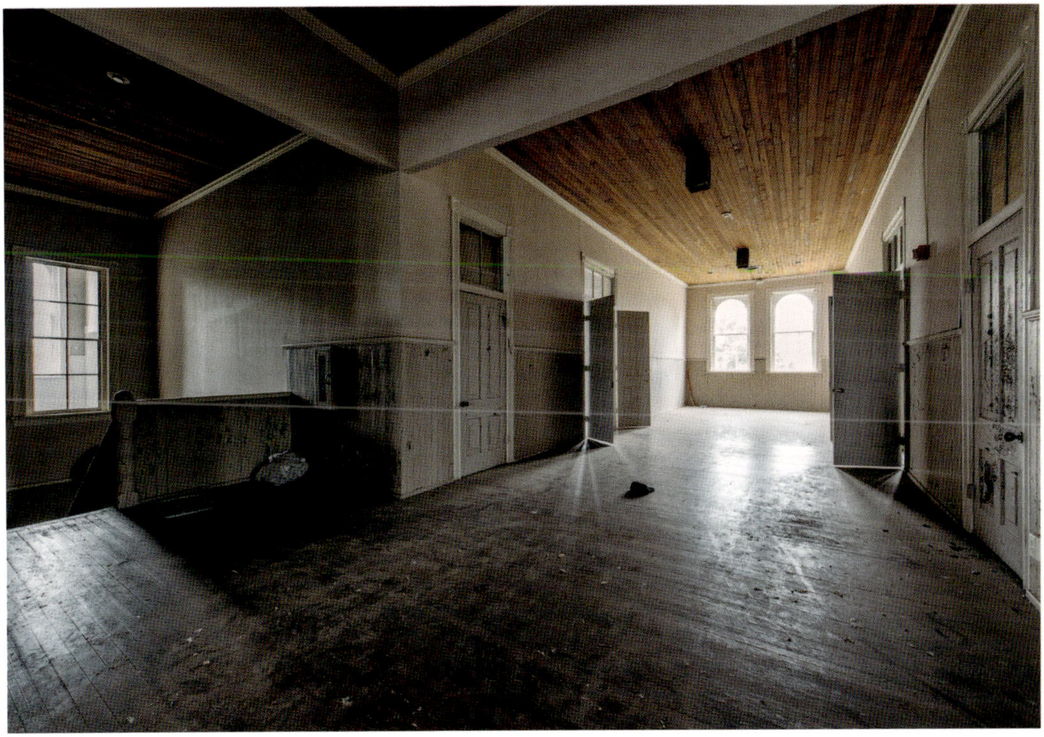

Another view of the second-floor hallway.

9

GOVERNOR'S HOUSE HOTEL

Located in Montgomery, the Governor's House Hotel was built in 1965 as a luxury hotel by C. T. Fitzpatrick, who also owned Empire-Rouse Laundry. It featured 197 rooms, over 19,500 square feet of meeting and convention space, the Rotunda restaurant, the Filibuster Lounge, and an outdoor pool in the shape of the state of Alabama. Planned with all the luxuries of a private country club, they also offered outdoor activities that other hotels in the area didn't, such as a nine-hole golf course and horseback riding.

The Governor's House Hotel was host to many prominent figures, such as former Alabama governors George Wallace and Fob James, who both held their campaign election parties in the Alabama Room. The cast and crew of the 1990 movie, *The Long Walk Home*, starring Whoopi Goldberg and Sissy Spacek, were also guests at the hotel.

In the late 1990s, the area had fallen into decline and the Governor's House Hotel was no longer the luxurious hotel it once was. By this time as well, travelers had much better hotel options in downtown Montgomery. The hotel was passed around to various owners, operating under various brands such as Motel 6 and Quality Inn & Suites. A Super 8 motel operated behind the old hotel, which was also abandoned around the same time.

Events were being held there as late as 2010. It was put up for auction in the early 2010s, but has since fallen into disrepair. Throughout the years, firefighters have responded to multiple fires at the property. In March 2017, firefighters put out a small fire that started in one of the rooms. Months later, two rooms on the second floor were damaged by another fire. In April 2019, firefighters responded to yet another fire which caused heavy damages to the interior of the building.

The Department of Revenue is currently in possession of the property due to unpaid property taxes. Although it's valued at $1 million, the first person to offer a minimum of $166,000 will be able to own the Governor's House Hotel.

There is no fence keeping people out so many homeless people have made it their home. What was once a luxurious hotel is now an eyesore with its windows shattered and graffiti covering its walls. Its once manicured grounds are now overgrown and filled with trash.

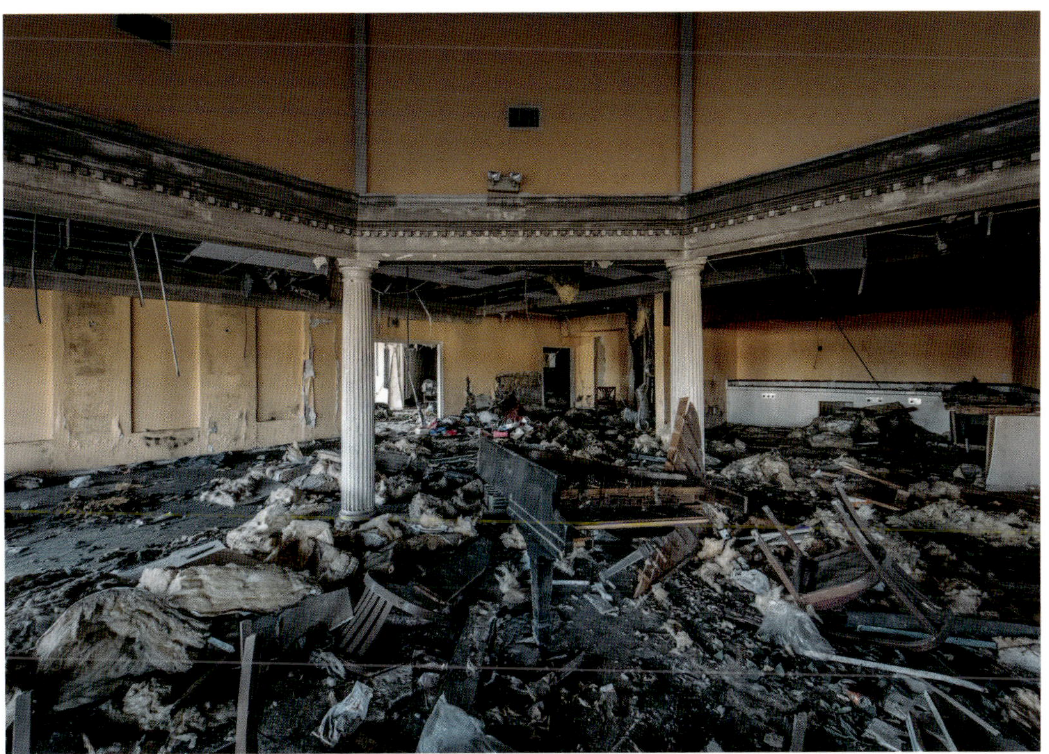

Inside of what remains of the Rotunda Restaurant.

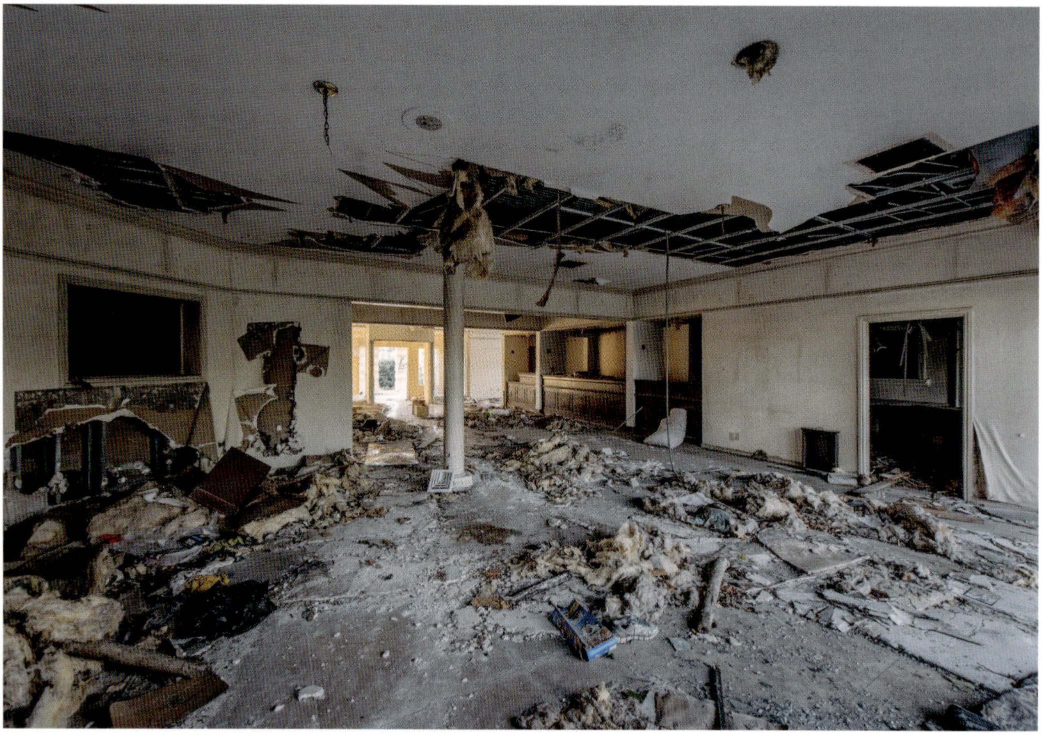

A look at the front reception desk.

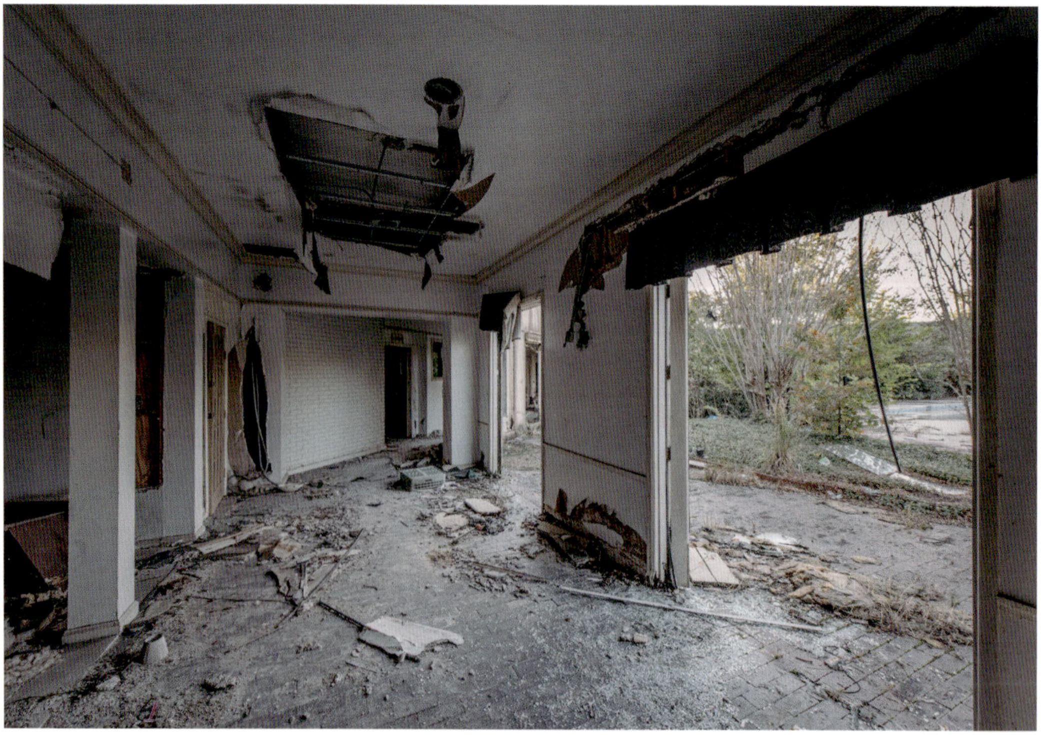

The hotel has been closed since at least 2010, as events were still being held here during that time.

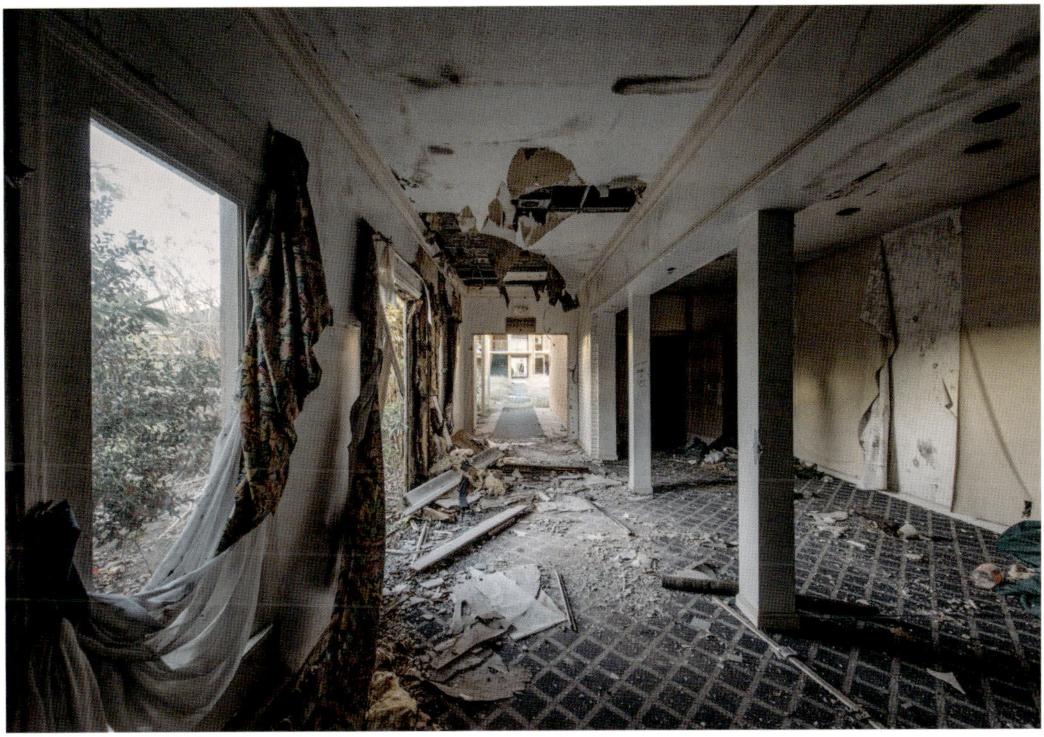

Smashed windows and curtains are strewn about this hallway.

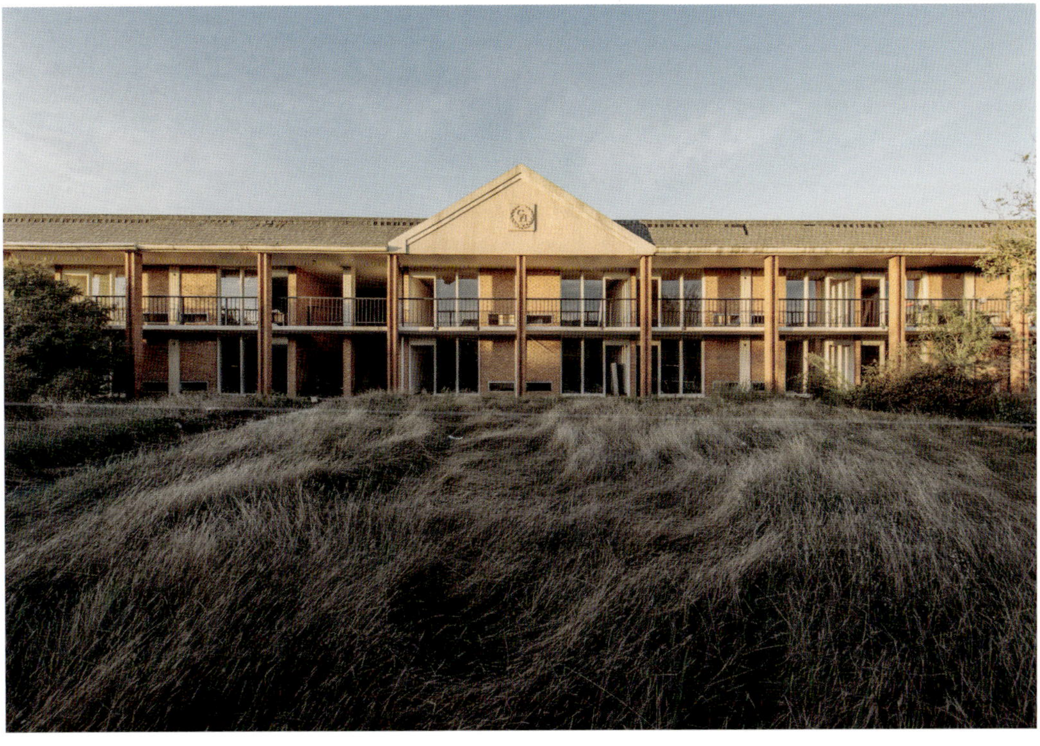

The back motel portion, which was a later addition to the Governor's House Hotel.

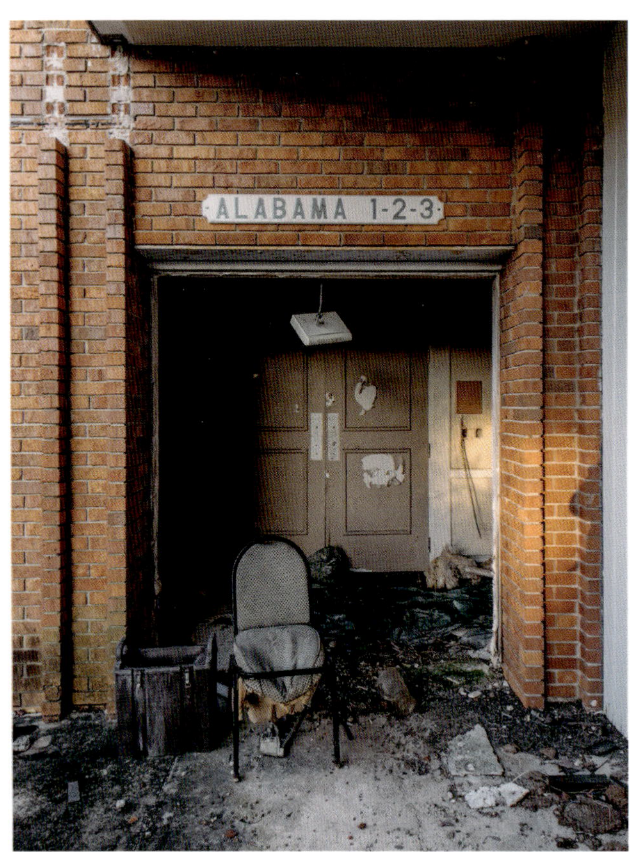

Left: Main entrance to the Alabama Room.

Below: A side to the Alabama Room used during events.

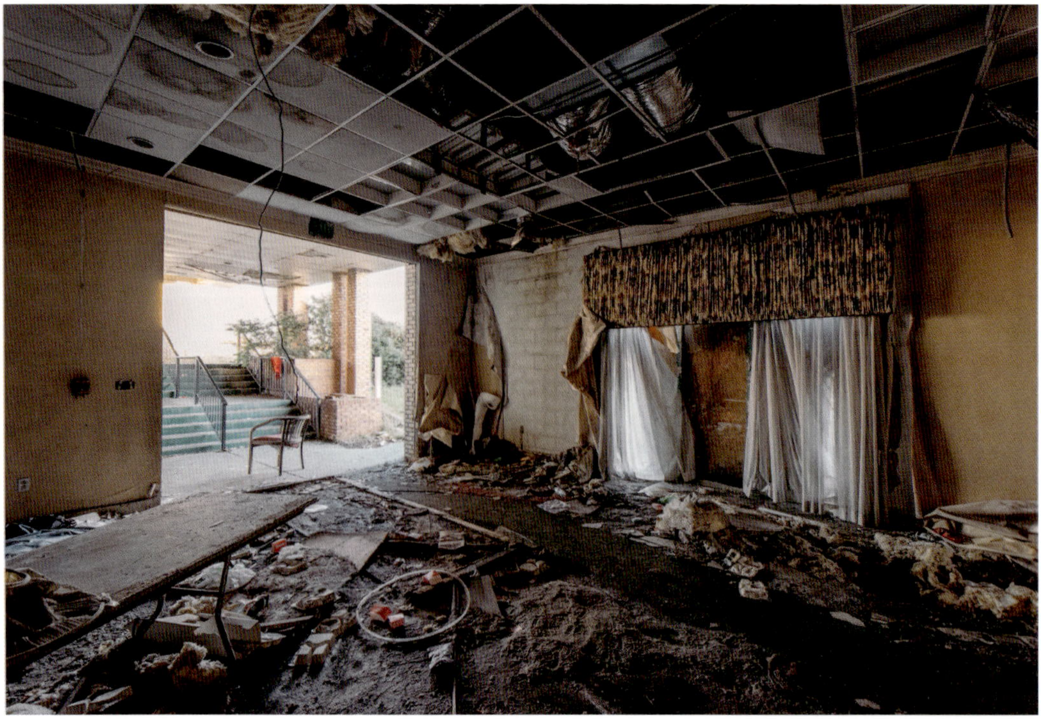

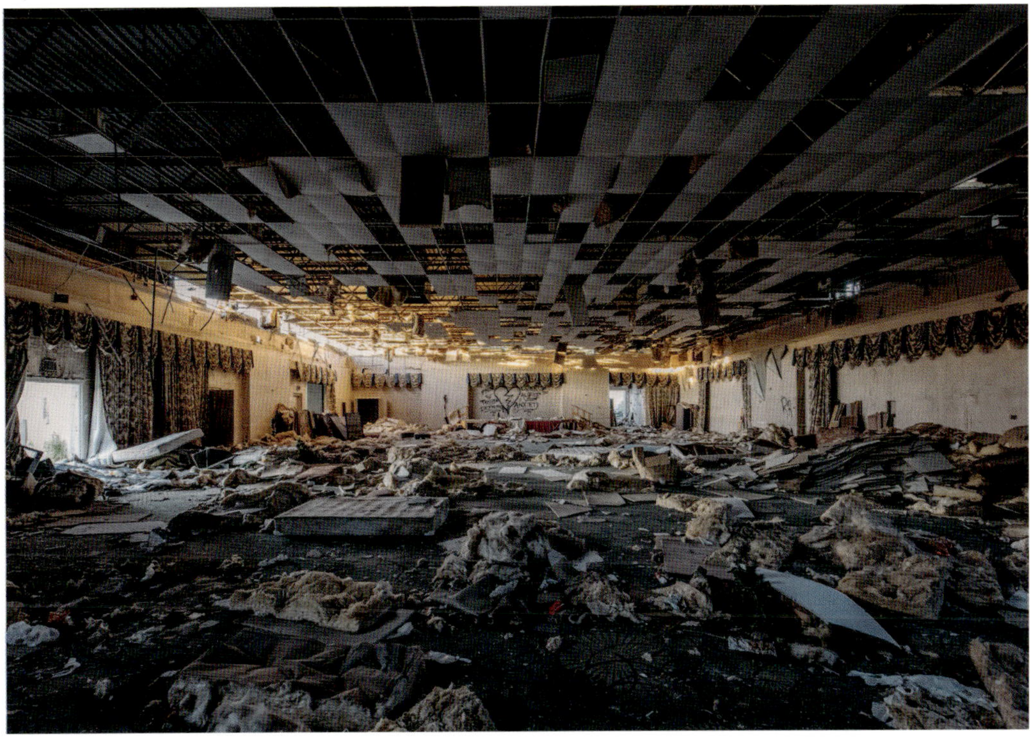

The Alabama Room played host to many election parties, dances, graduations, and other events.

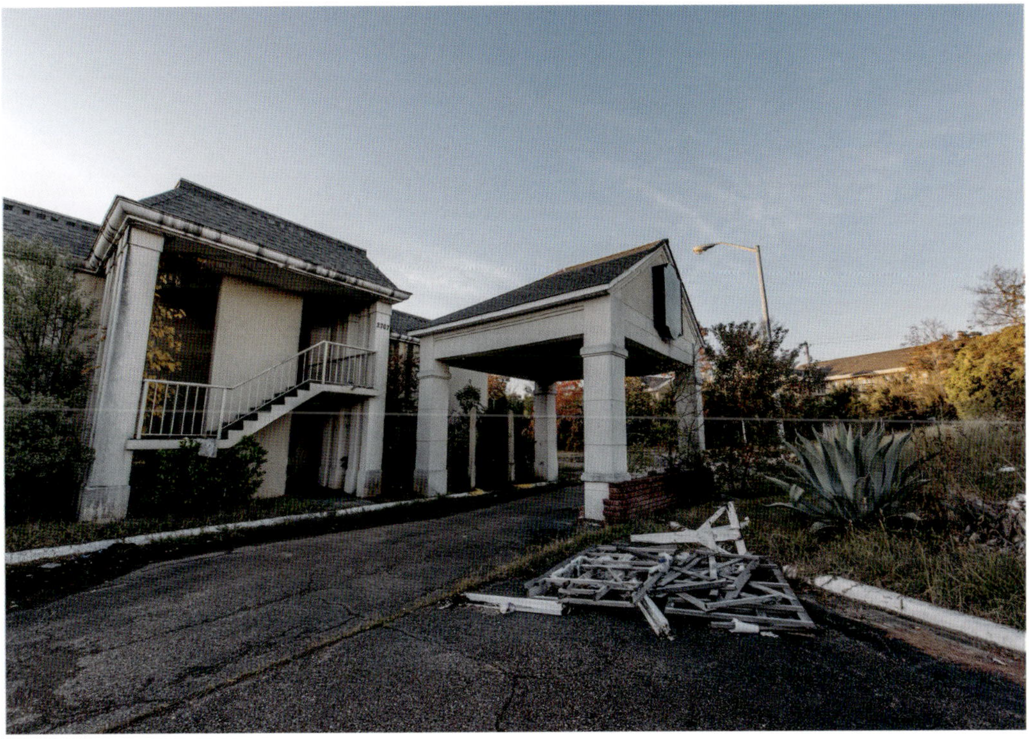

Around back was a Super 8 Motel, abandoned around the same time as the Governor's House Hotel.

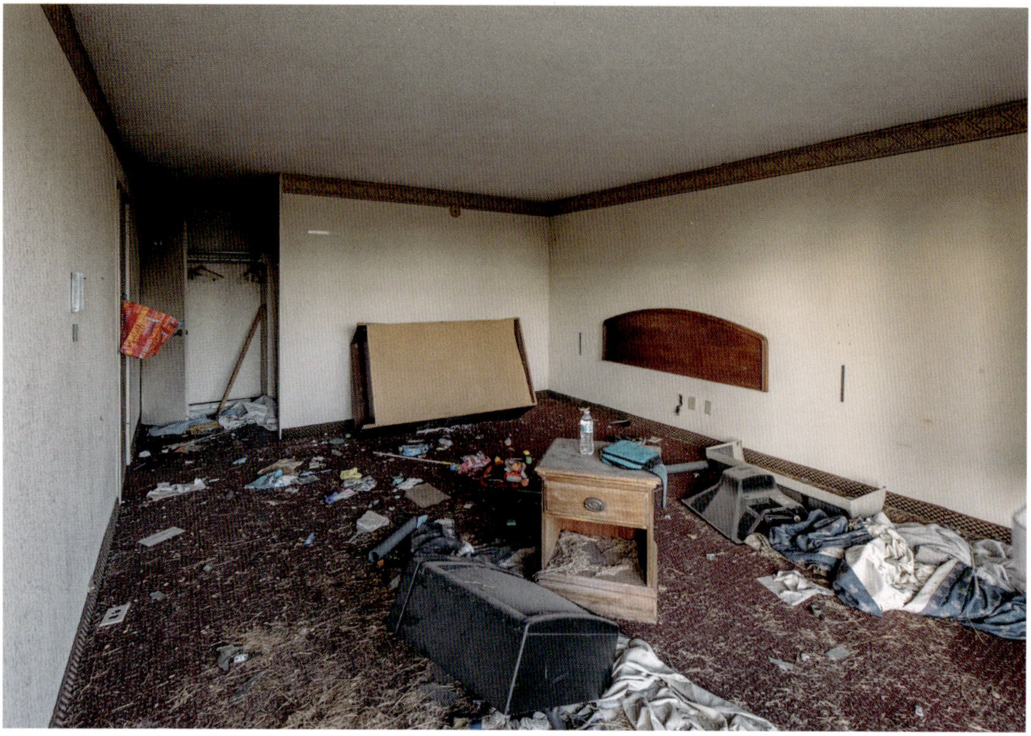

Garbage and human waste litter the floor.

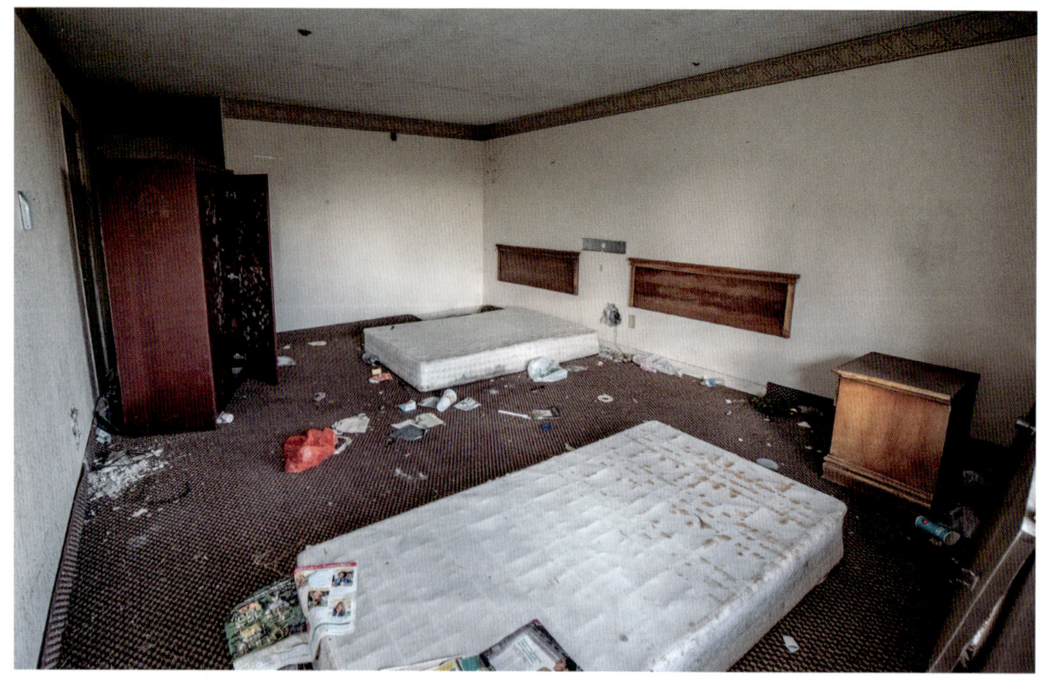

Weeks after shooting here, someone cleaned up the property, clearing out hundreds of pounds of garbage.

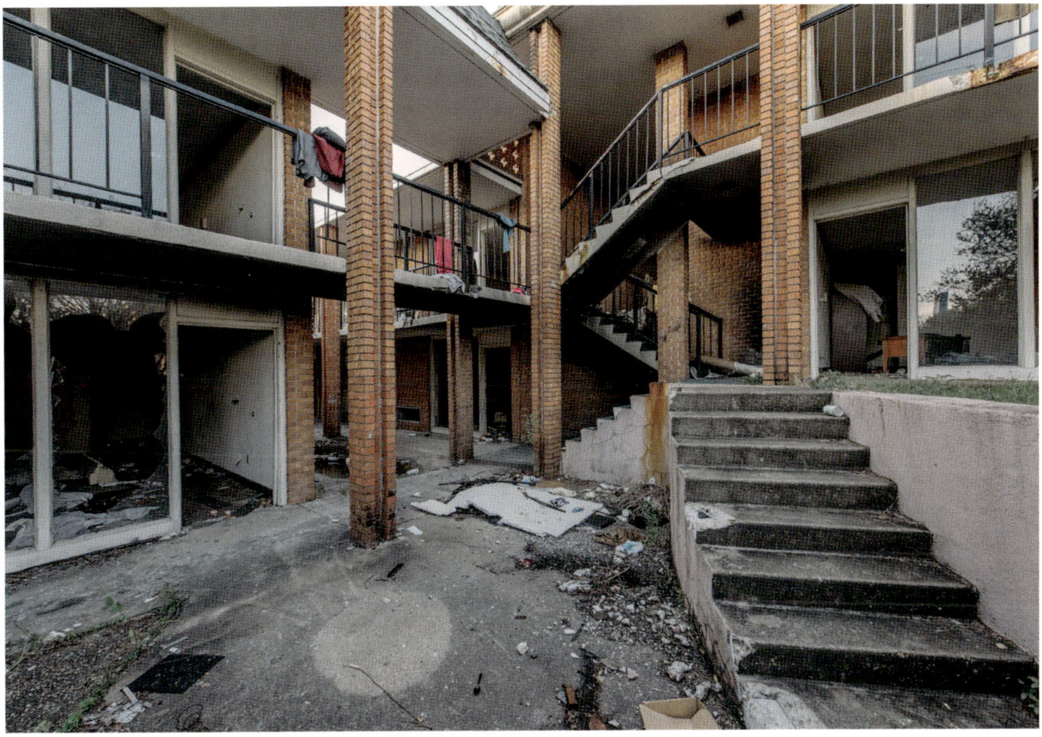

Clothing possibly once owned by a homeless person is strewn about the property and hanging from balcony railings.

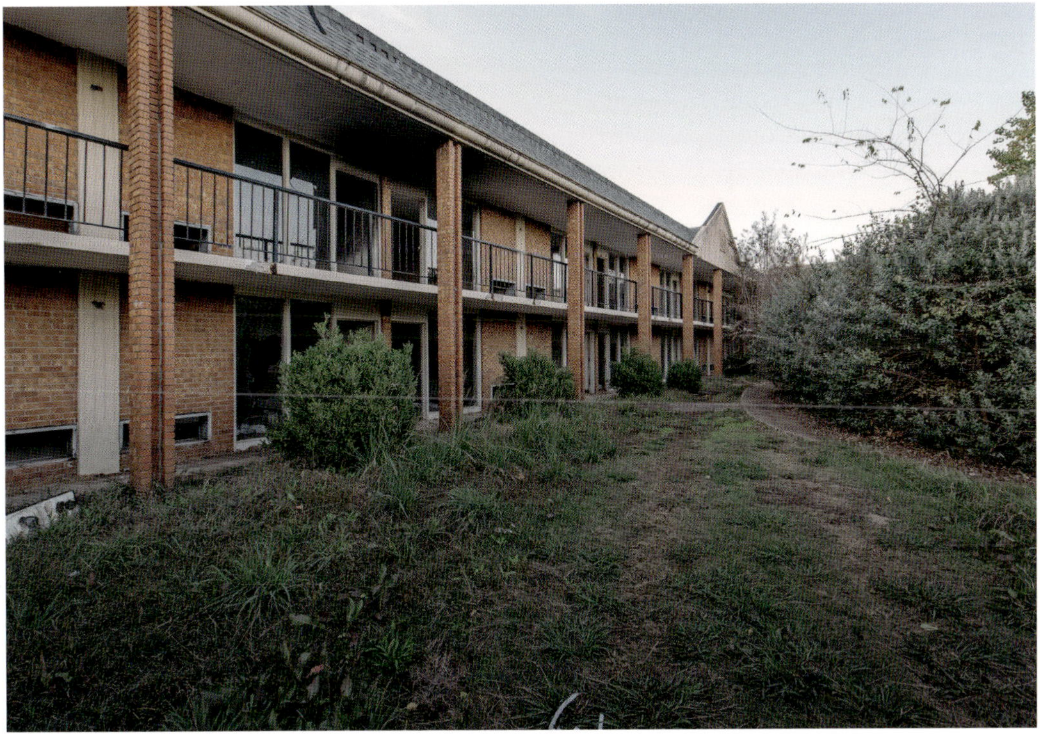

Another look at the back portion of the hotel containing a building which served as a motel.

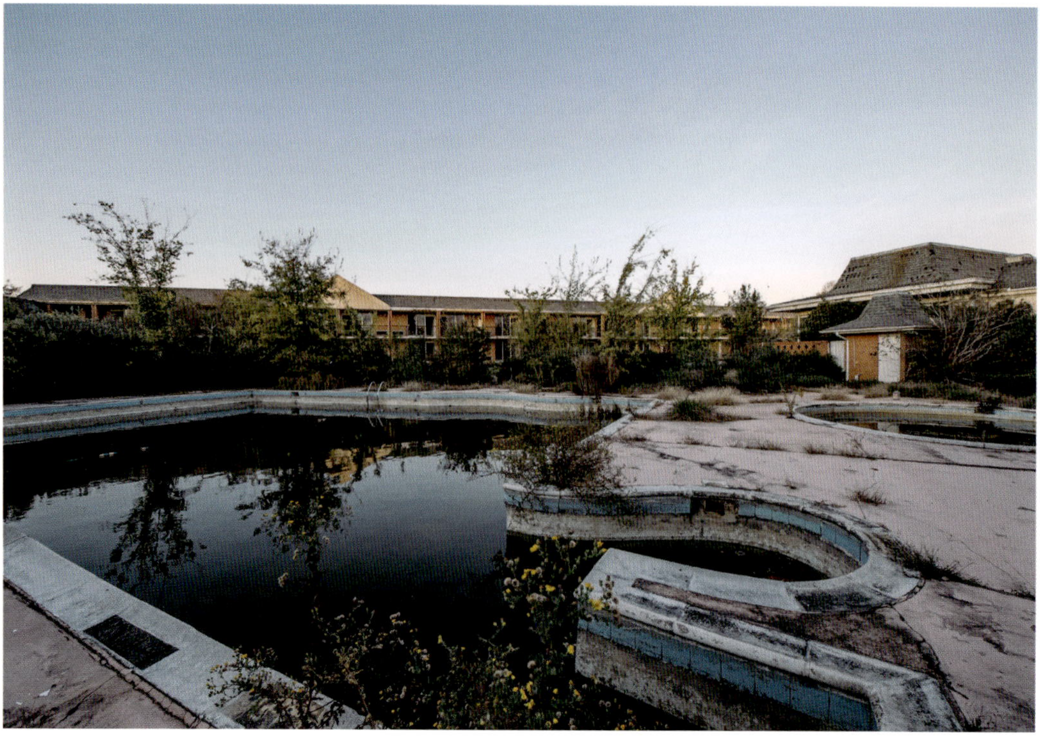

The pool is shaped like the state of Alabama.

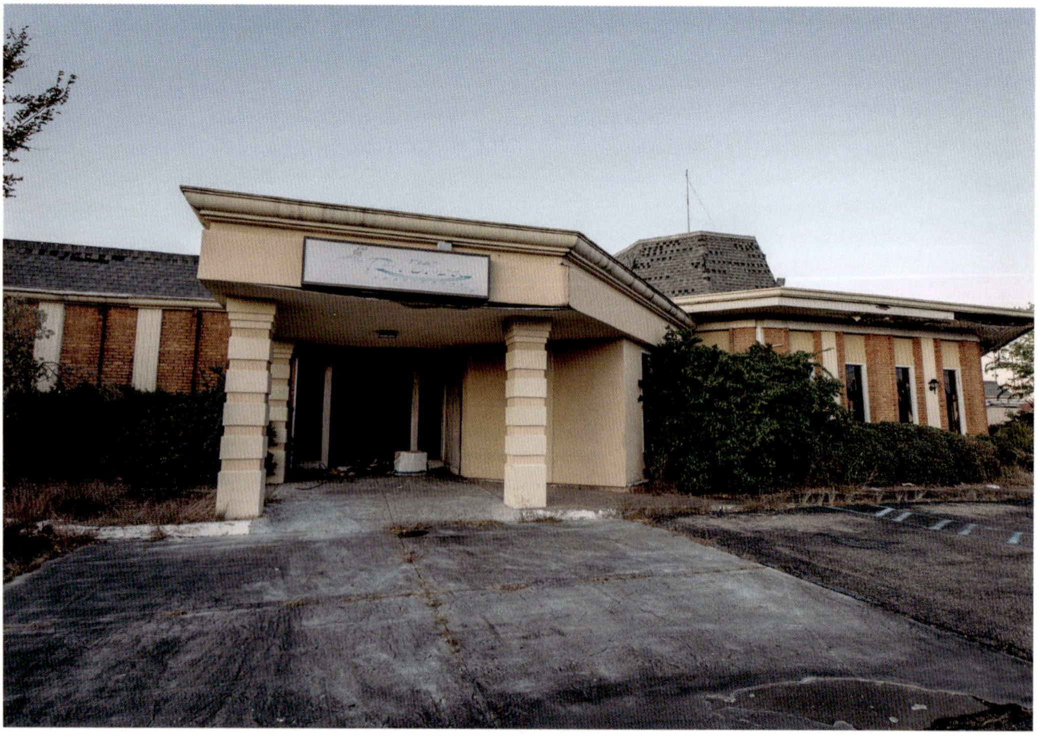

One can sort of make out the sign which reads "The Rotunda Restaurant."

10

PENNY PROFIT MEAT MARKET

The Penny Profit and Discount Meat Market was a small corner market owned by Rubin and Julia Hanan, well-known around Montgomery for their charcoal seasonings. Rubin emigrated from Greece to the United States in 1925, winding up in Montgomery to pursue an education. He ended up meeting Julia Cohen, and they would get married in 1935 in a traditional Sephardic ceremony. The newlywed couple moved to Atlanta, but after their eight-month-old infant daughter died, they moved back to Montgomery to start anew. It was at this time that they opened the Hull Street Market, operating it solely as a butcher shop.

Where the current building now stands was once the site of a small A&P grocery store. A&P was a national chain of grocery stores specializing in tea and coffee, eventually becoming the largest food retailer in the United States in the 1920s. In the late 1930s, A&P began shifting from small corner markets and combination stores to the much larger and more efficient supermarkets.

In 1937, A&P opened a new supermarket across from its original location, selling the building to Rubin Hanan. The Hanans struggled to compete with their big-chain neighbor, so to differentiate themselves, they invented charcoal seasoning. They became renowned throughout Montgomery for their charcoal-blackened steaks.

In 1950, the old market was replaced with a more modern building, which included a freezer and refrigeration units. Renamed to the Penny Profit and Discount Meat Market, Rubin and Julia Hanan found great success in the business. Rubin became politically involved, especially with issues involving senior citizens, becoming a delegate to the White House Conference on Aging in 1961 and 1971, and was appointed by President Lyndon B. Johnson to the Advisory Committee for Older Americans in 1965. Julia was renowned for her cooking, eventually publishing a cookbook, *Dulce Siempre*, in 2001.

The Hanans were getting old and Rubin's health was declining, so a decision was made to sell the business, including the charcoal-seasoning recipe they became known for. The business was sold to the Landers family's patriarch along with a business partner of his. Unfortunately, it wasn't long before the two partners split off, and the Penny Profit closed in the early 2000s.

Rubin Hanan died in 1996. Julia moved to Birmingham to be with her family, where she would pass away in 2005. The building has remained closed since then, sitting across from the long-shuttered A&P supermarket. The original charcoal, however, continues on, sold by the Landers family under the name, "Mis' Rubin's Black Magic."

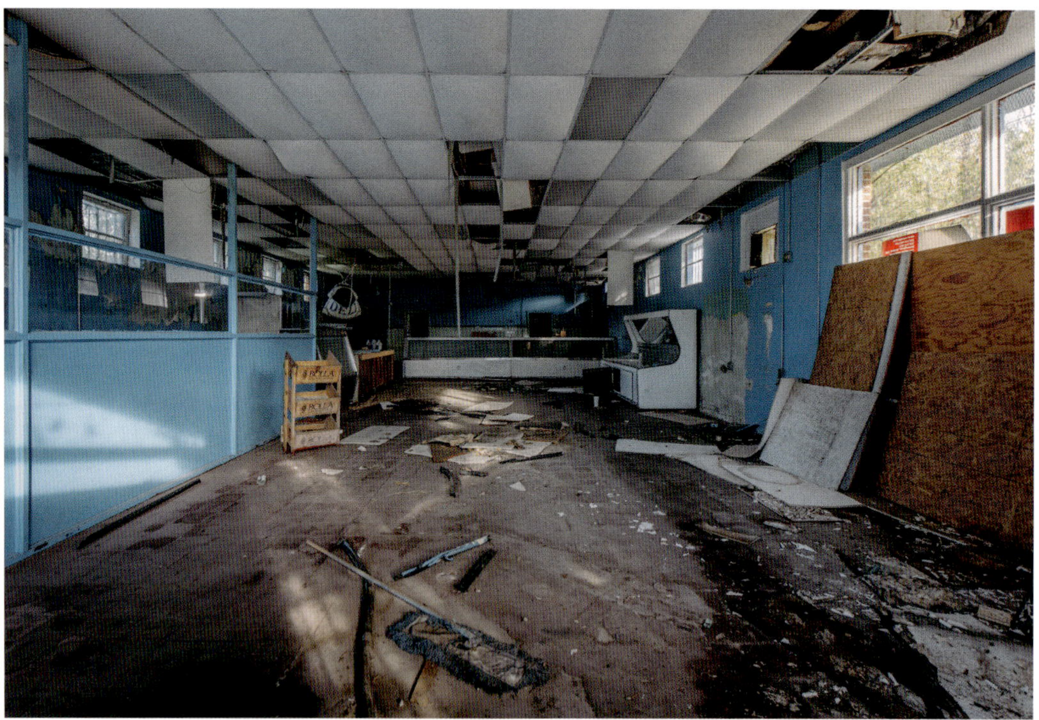

Inside the former Penny Profit Meat Market.

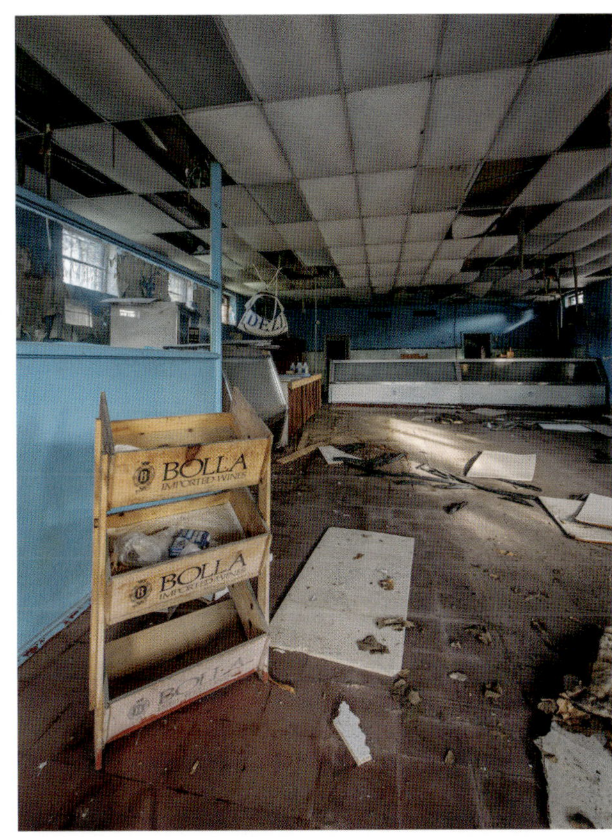

Right: A stand which held bottles of wine.

Below: A look at the deli and meat counter.

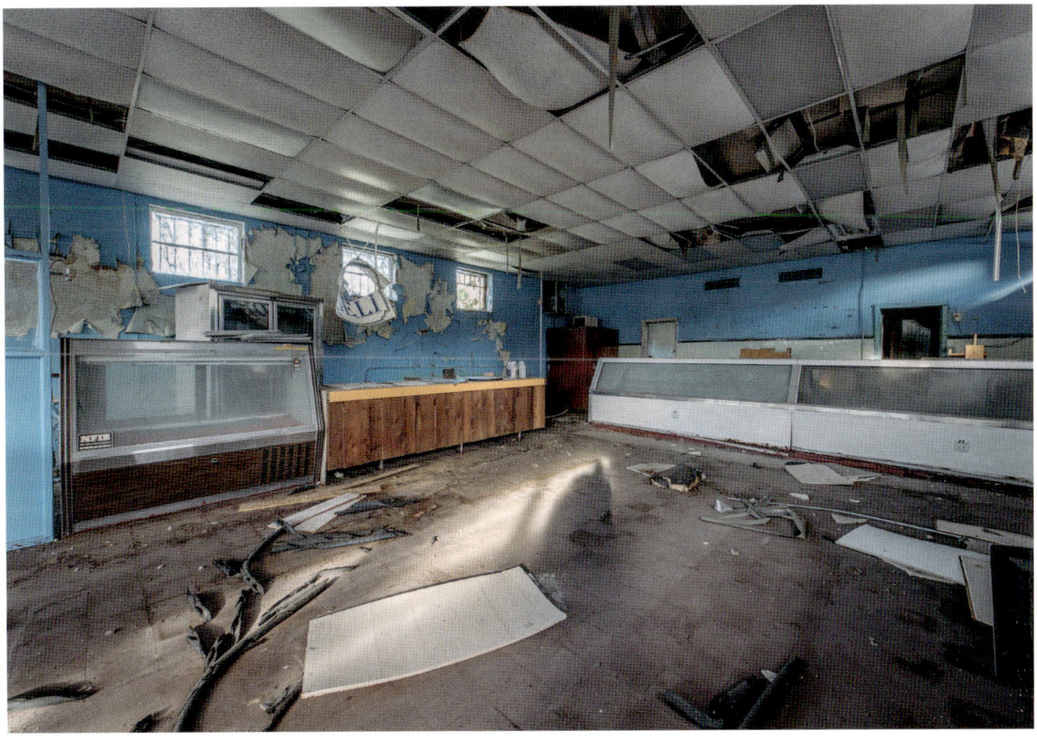

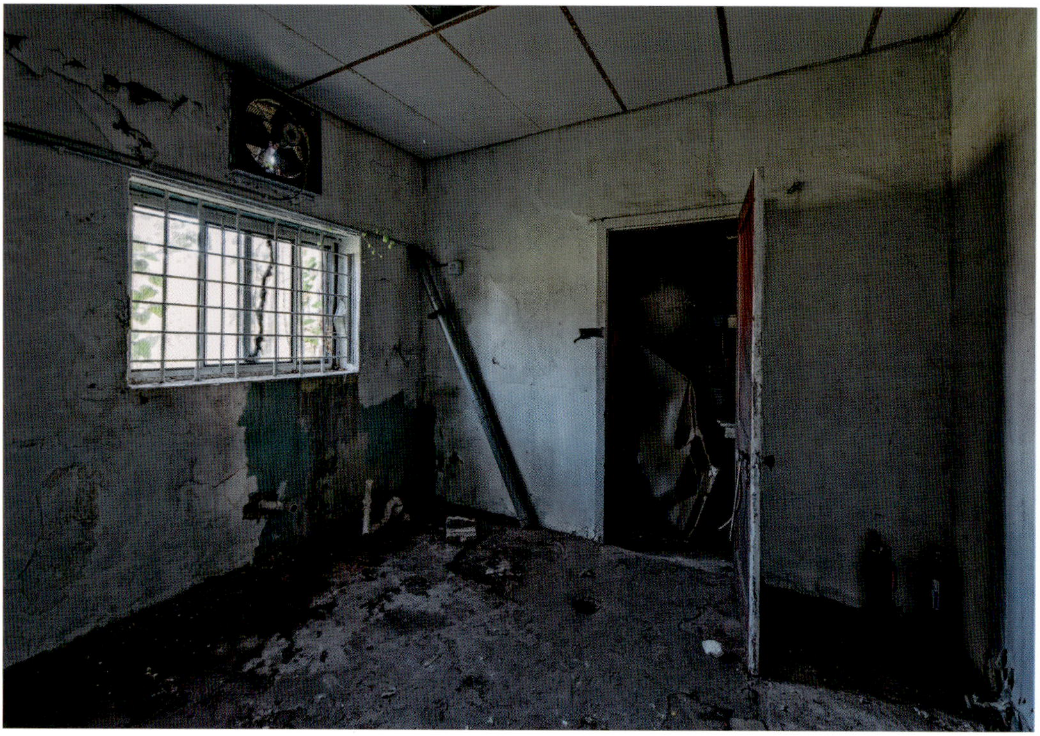

Inside the freezer in the rear of the building.

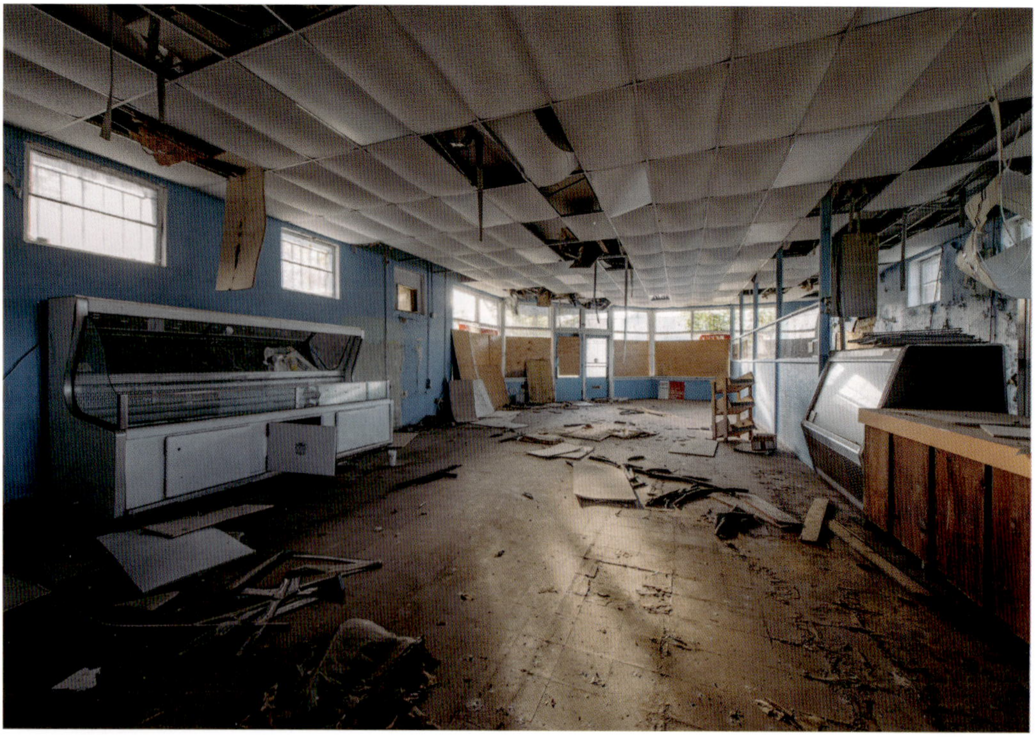

Looking out towards the front of the building.

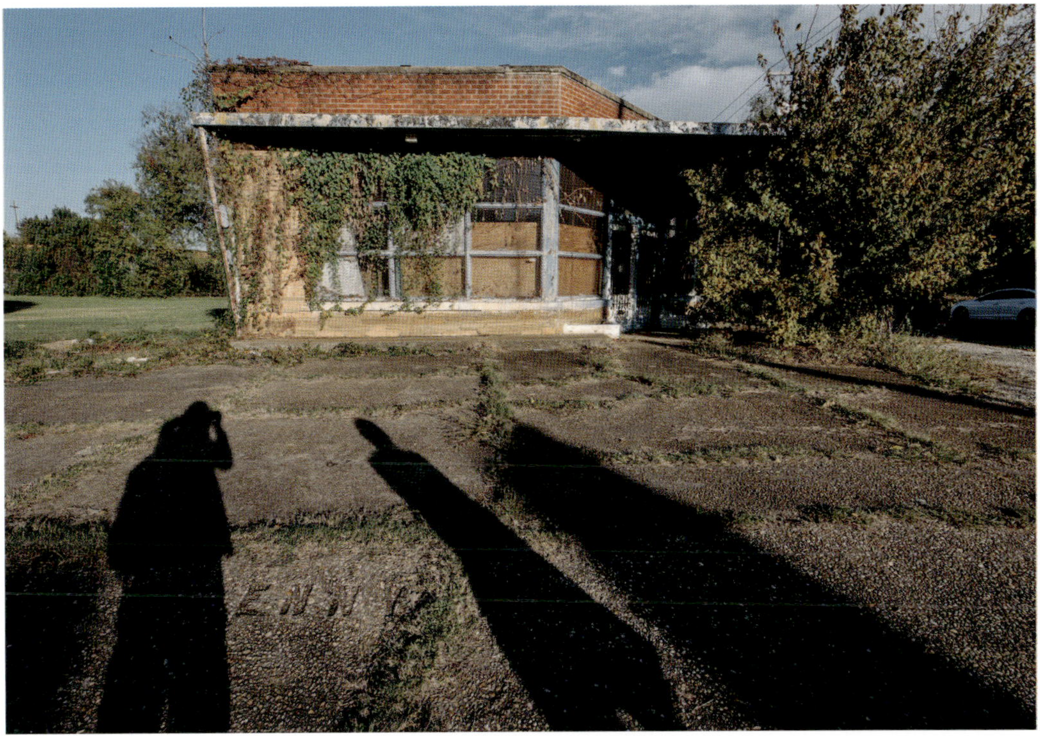

Above: The words "PENNY PROFIT" can be made out etched into the concrete in the bottom of this photo.

Right: A sign reads "Penny Profit Customer Parking Only."

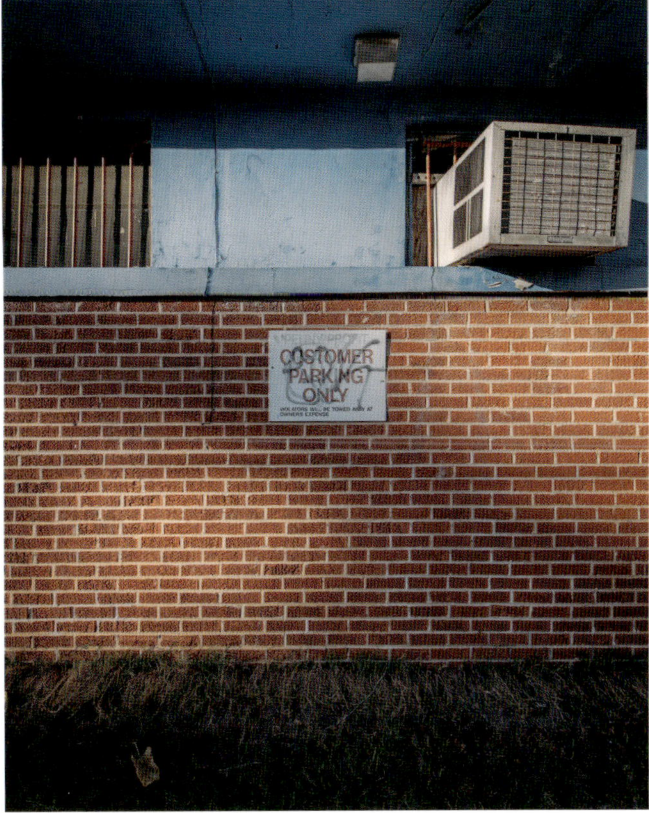

11

W.B. PATERSON ELEMENTARY SCHOOL

William Burns Paterson is known for being an educational provider and one of the founders of Alabama State University. Born on February 9, 1850, in Scotland, he made his way to America in 1867 and drifted his way down south, eventually opening a school for negroes in early 1870. He moved the school to a log cabin located four miles outside of Greensboro before settling in a small frame structure he constructed himself in Greensboro in 1871. Paterson named the school Tullibody Academy, after his home village back in Scotland and remained at the school until 1878 when he moved to Marion. Tullibody Academy operated until 1886 with help and financial aid of many affluent members of the community, despite opposition from many whites in Greensboro who were indifferent or hostile towards Negro education.

In 1879, Paterson became president of the Lincoln Normal University for Colored Students, where he remained for many years. In 1887, Paterson began working on securing an appropriation as well as a legislative authorization to relocate the school after a fire destroyed many of the campus buildings. In 1889, the school was relocated to Montgomery, where he reopened it in the Beulah Baptist church under the name of State Normal School for Colored Students. Paterson presided over the institution until he died of heart failure on March 16, 1915. The name of the institution would change throughout the following years until 1969, when the State Board of Education, then the governing body of the university, had the name changed to Alabama State University.

Bearing his name, W. B. Paterson Elementary School was first constructed in 1953 at a cost of precisely $227,527.63, consisting of twelve classrooms, a multi-purpose room with a stage and kitchen, offices, medical clinic, and a teacher's lounge. The building was expanded throughout the years with daily attendance peaking in the early-1960s with over 760 students, some of which were children of military and civilian personnel stationed at the nearby Maxwell Air Force Base, Gunter Air Force Base, and Veteran's Administration Hospital.

Paterson Elementary, like many schools in Alabama at the time, was segregated, and exclusively black children were in attendance. After the United States Supreme Court's 1954 ruling in Brown v. Board of Education struck down racial segregation in public schools, the Alabama legislature followed up by passing a constitutional amendment in 1956 that eliminated the state's responsibility to guarantee public education. This amendment was designed to avoid desegregation and provide support for segregated private schools, which soon began appearing all throughout the state. This amendment also allowed any school to suddenly close down when faced with integration. It wasn't until the late 1960s, with the passing of the Civil Rights Act in 1964 and then in 1967, the invalidation of a 1955 "pupil placement law" by U.S. District Judge Frank M. Johnson Jr., did integration truly begin in Alabama's school system.

Paterson Elementary School closed down in 2009 following a vote by the Montgomery County Board of Education. Two other schools in the county, Hayneville Road Elementary School and Pintlala Elementary School, were closed along with it in an effort to save $3 million for a school system facing a $13 million revenue shortfall. At the time of its closing, Paterson Elementary served 153 students from K-5th grade with a student to teacher ratio of 10:1, one of the lowest in the state. The school reopened for a short time as Paterson Academy Creative Education, a magnet school serving grades 6-12, but that too was shuttered.

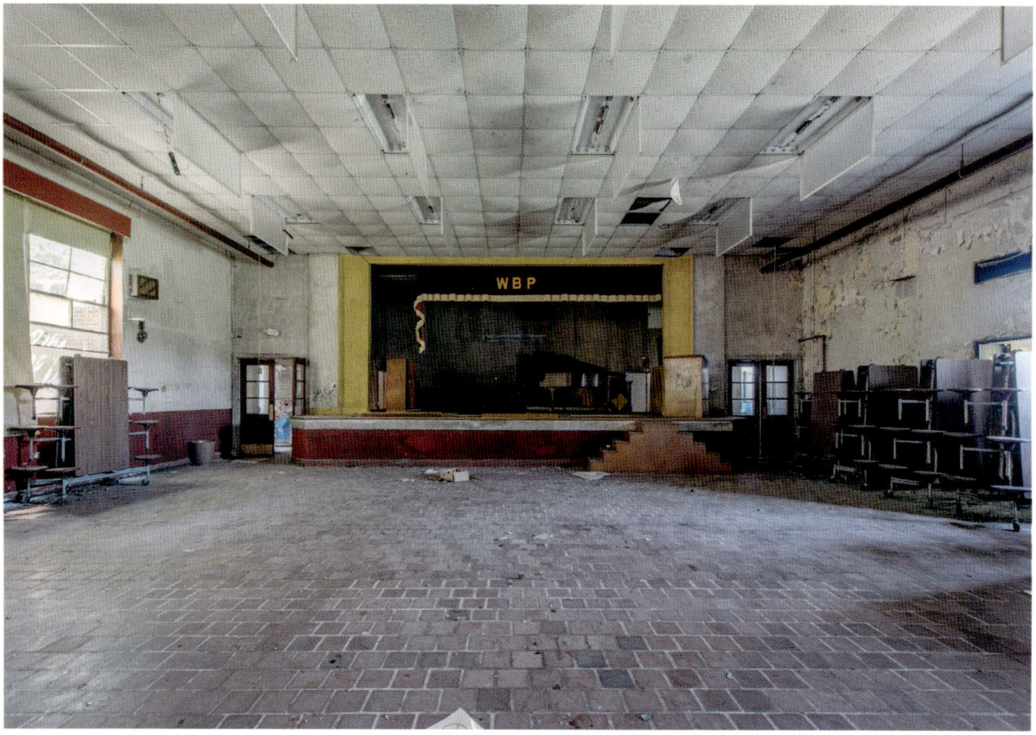

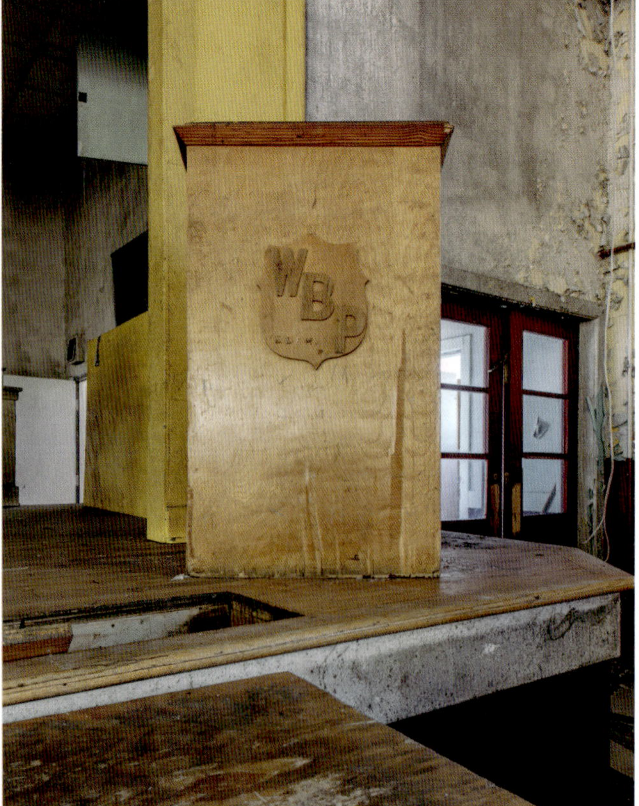

Above: The Lettering on the curtain reads "WBP," standing for William Burns Paterson.

Left: A podium on the stage of the auditorium with the letters "WBP" on it.

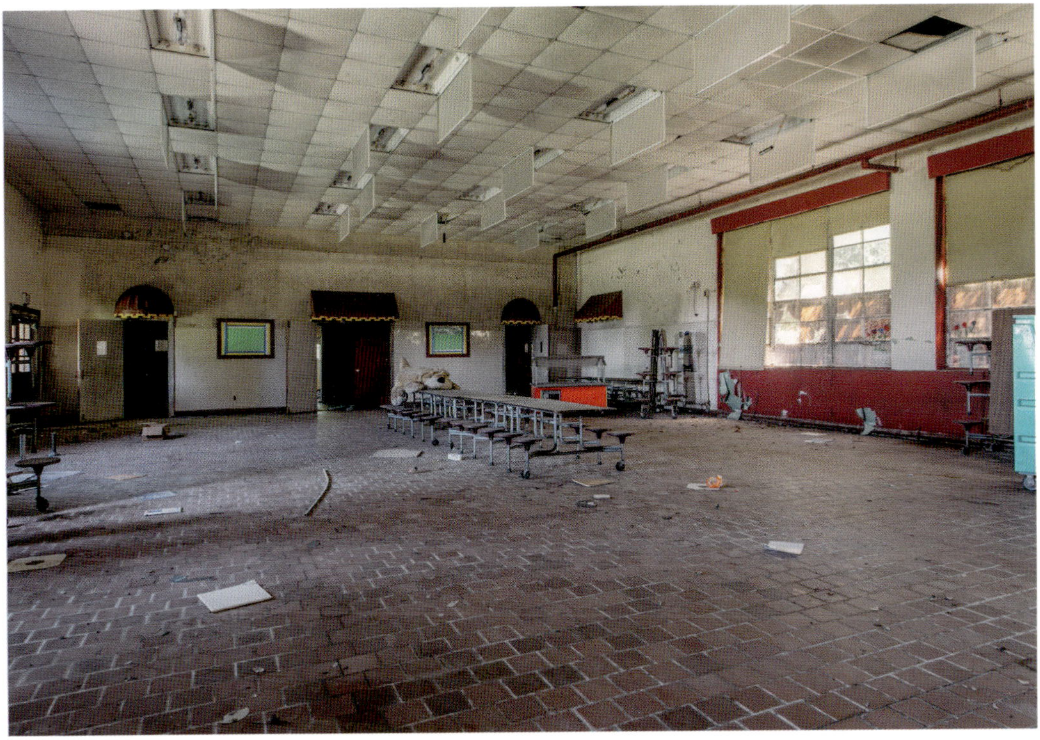

Another look of the cafeteria, which also served as the auditorium.

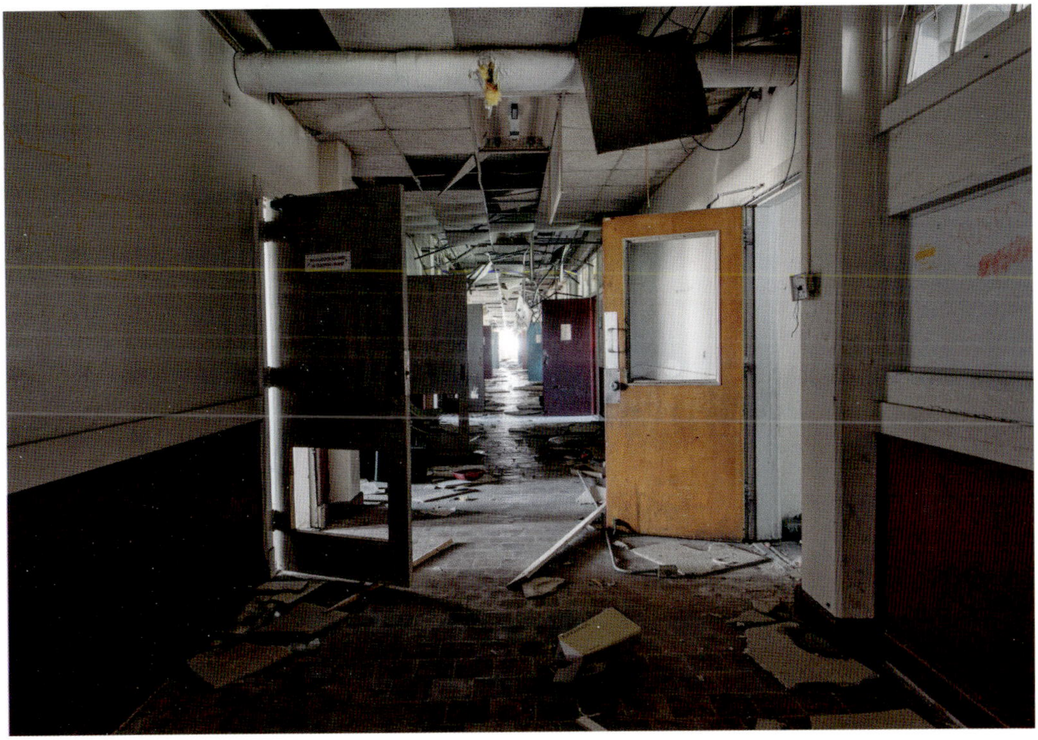

Much of the building is destroyed due to scrappers ripping out the metal within the walls.

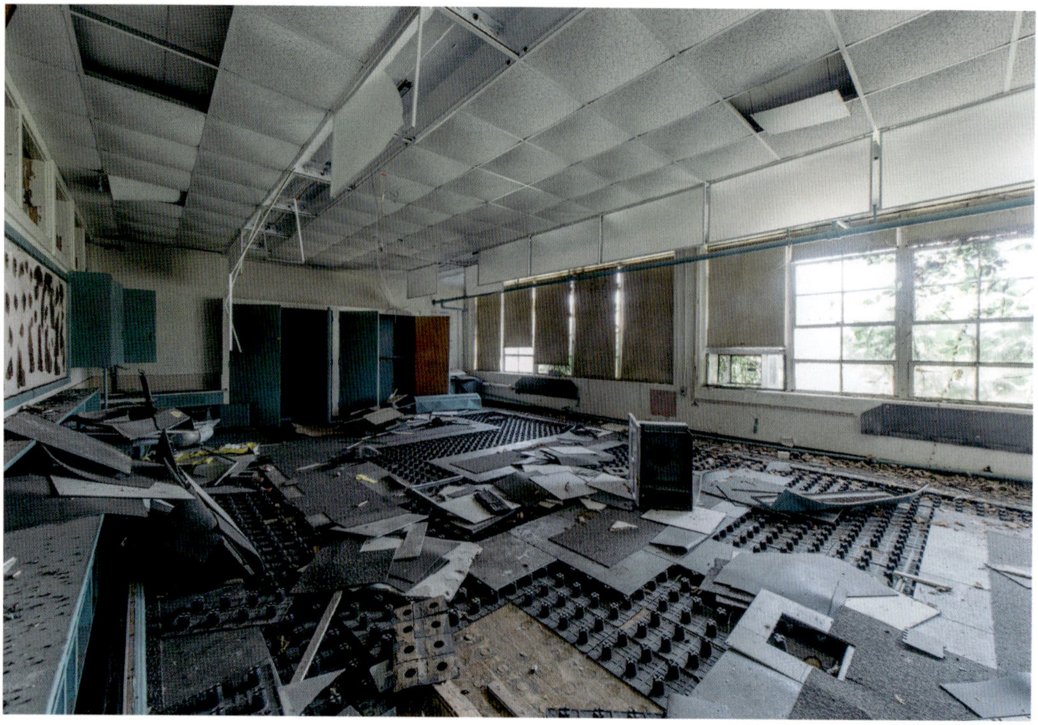

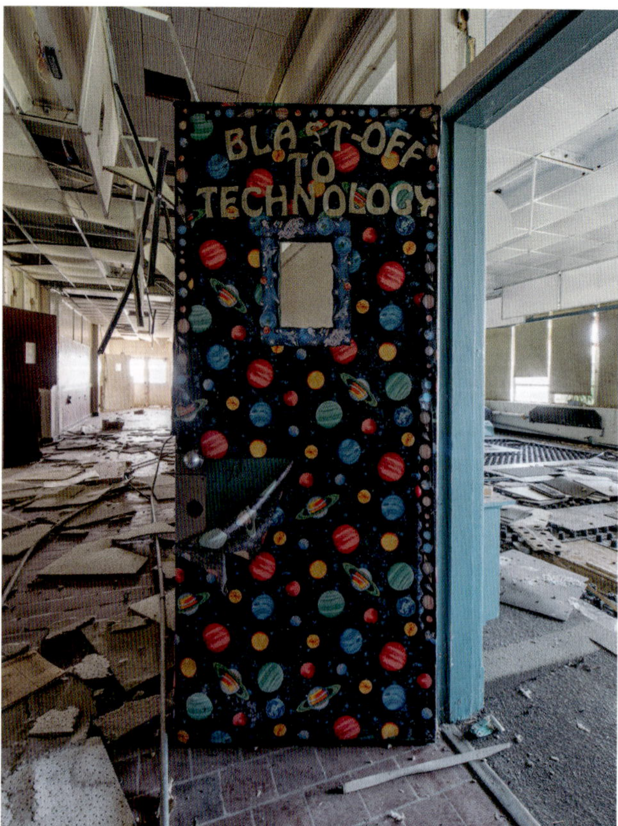

Above: The flooring here in the computer room is raised to allow cables to be run underneath the floor rather than having it be a risk.

Left: The door to the computer room is decorated in planets and reads, "Blast-Off to Technology."

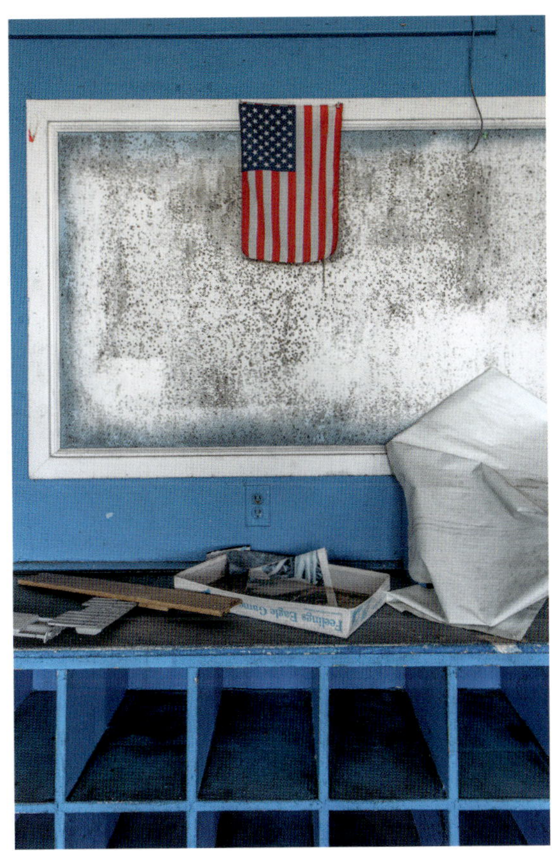

Right: A lone American flag hangs against a moldy wall.

Below: A game probably hasn't been played on this board in over a decade.

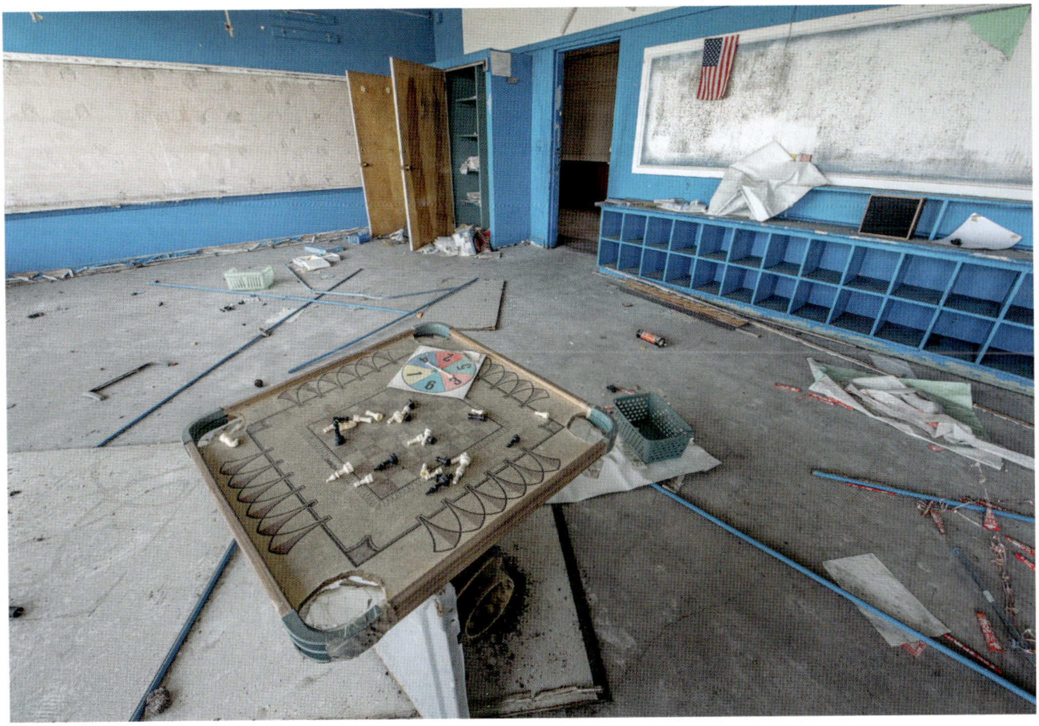

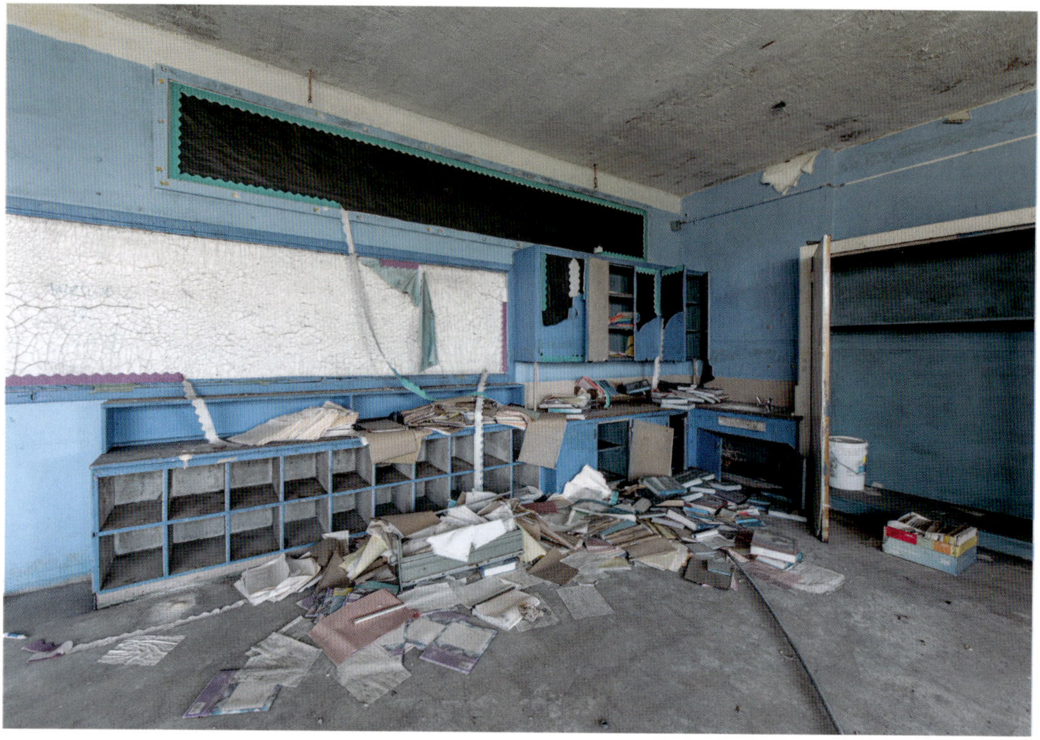

Hundreds of textbooks can be found throughout the building.

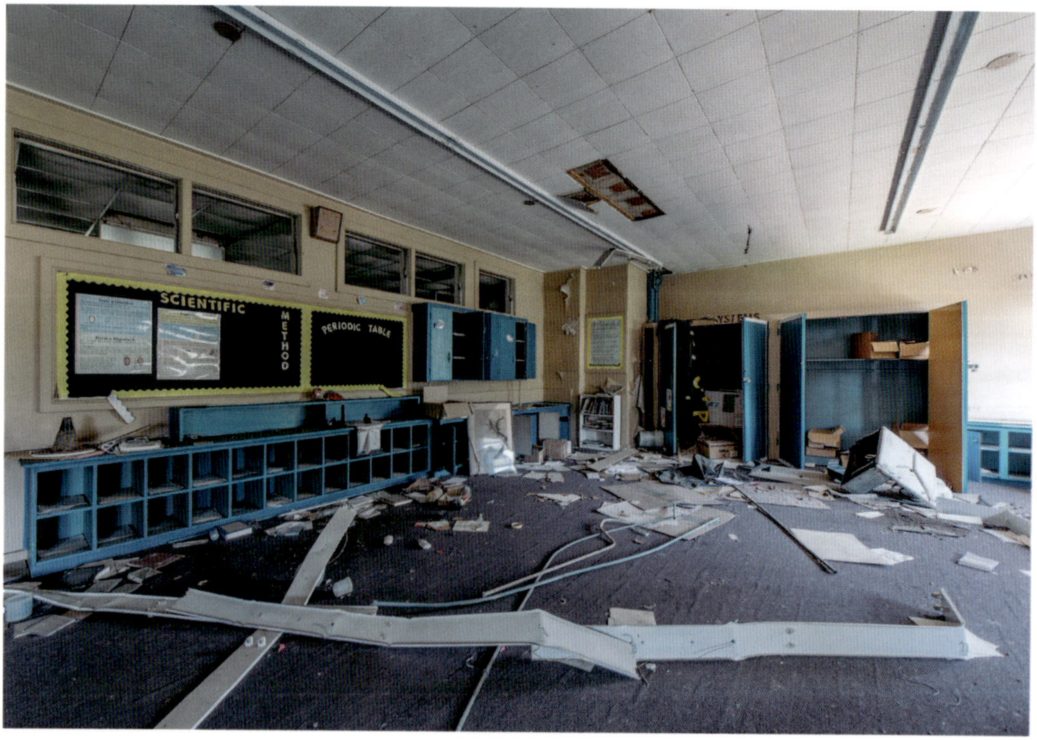

Inside the science classroom.

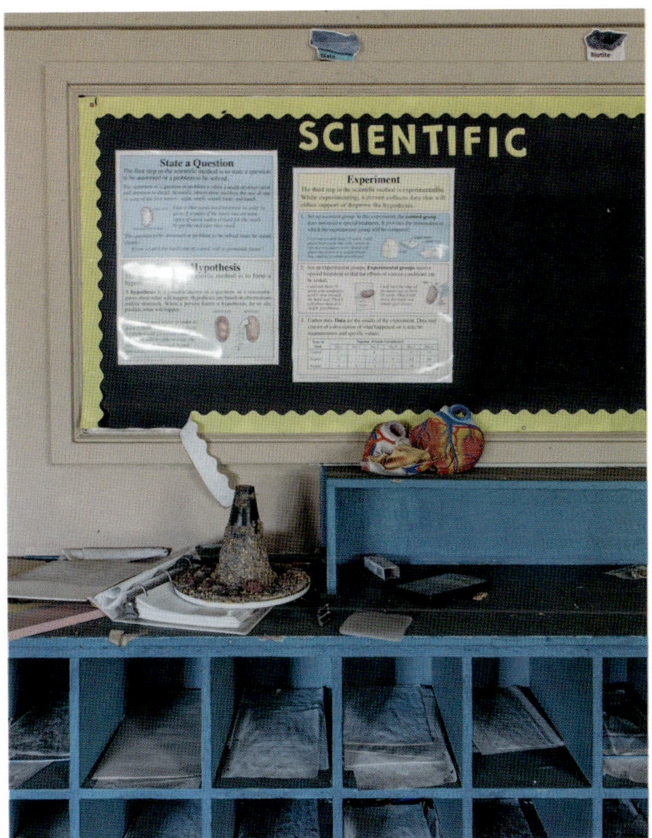

Right: A plastic heart and a volcano experiment sit underneath letters which read "Scientific."

Below: The school has been closed since 2009, over a decade ago.

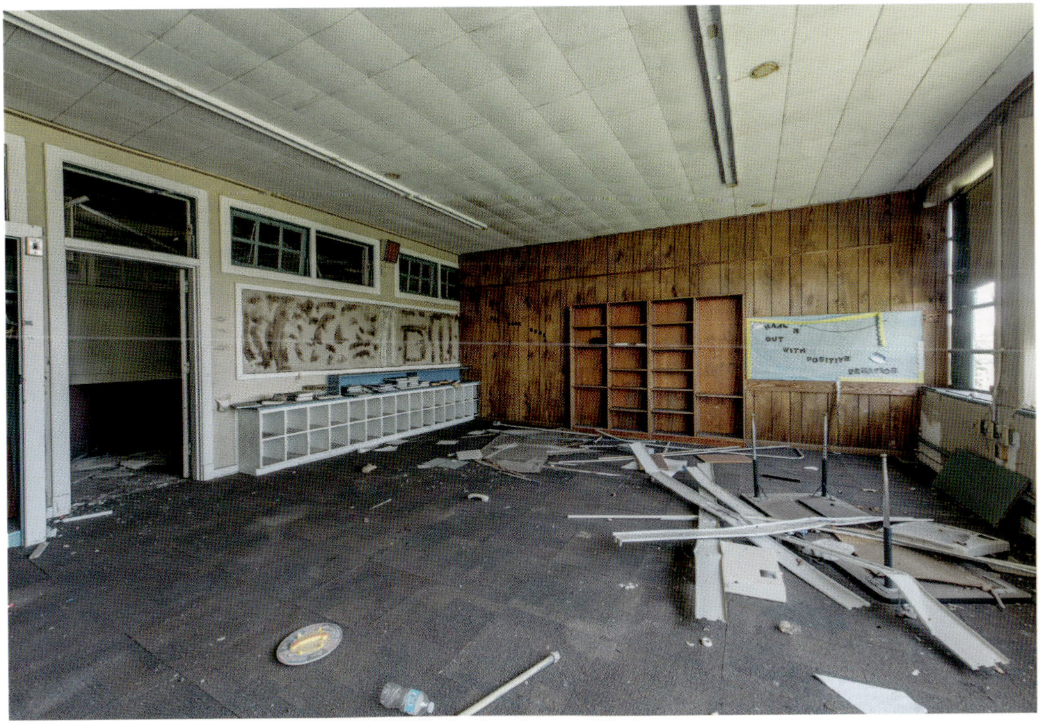

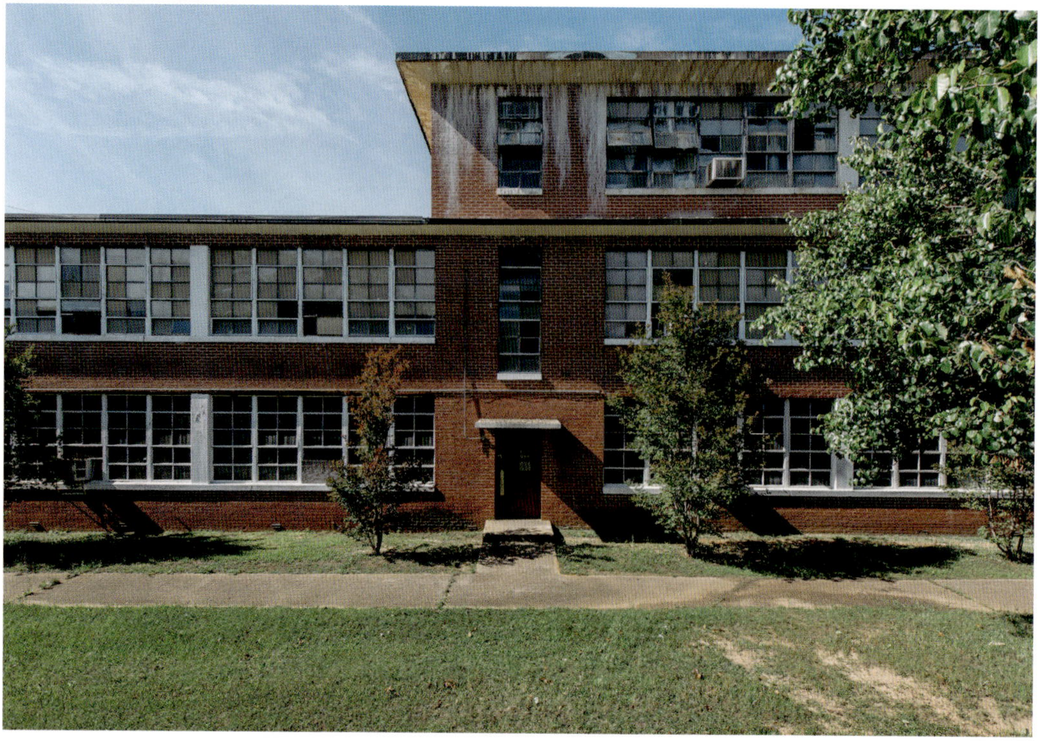

The building is looking its age due to the weather and lack of maintenance.

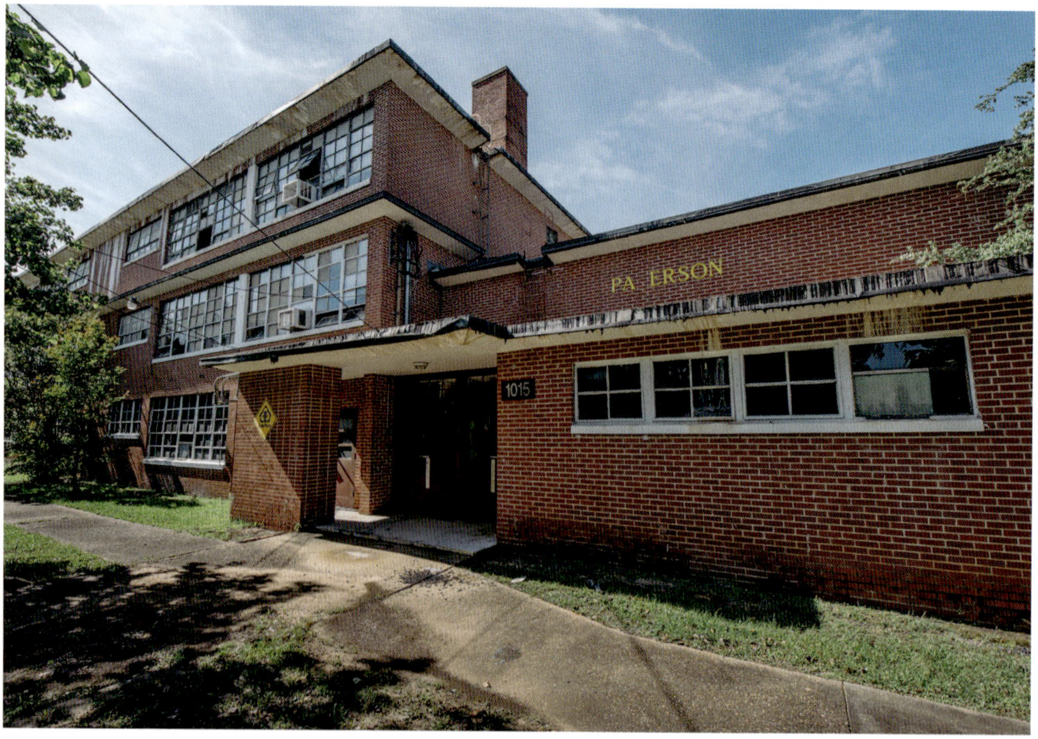

Lettering on the wall of the building which once read "Paterson."

12

KOPPERS INDUSTRIES WOOD TREATMENT FACILITY

Koppers Industries was a wood treating facility, primarily railroad ties, located near the downtown area of Montgomery. The facility was first constructed in 1925 under a joint venture by the Ayer and Lord Tie Company and the Bond Brothers Creosote Company with operations beginning in 1926 as Producers Wood Preserving. At the time, only creosote treatment was implemented, chemicals created by the high-temperature treatment of wood and fossil fuels such as oil.

Koppers Industries purchased the facility in 1941. Creosote treatment continued to be used until 1957 when it was replaced with pentachlorophenol (penta) treatment. The treatment was initially a mixture of creosote and penta known as creo-penta treatment, but it was replaced in 1962 with an oil-penta mixture, where penta is dissolved in diesel fuel. The oil-penta mixture was used up until the closure of the facility.

The facility was closed between 1982 and 1983, and the long process of cleaning up the property began. Supernatant and recoverable oils were pretreated on-site and then moved to a nearby public treatment plant. Any waste deemed hazardous was burned in an on-site boiler. The cooling and settlement ponds were filled in between 1989 and 1992. Few remnants remain of the facility, such as this administrative building located just outside of the main facility. Heavily vandalized and deteriorating, it won't be much longer until this building is torn down as well.

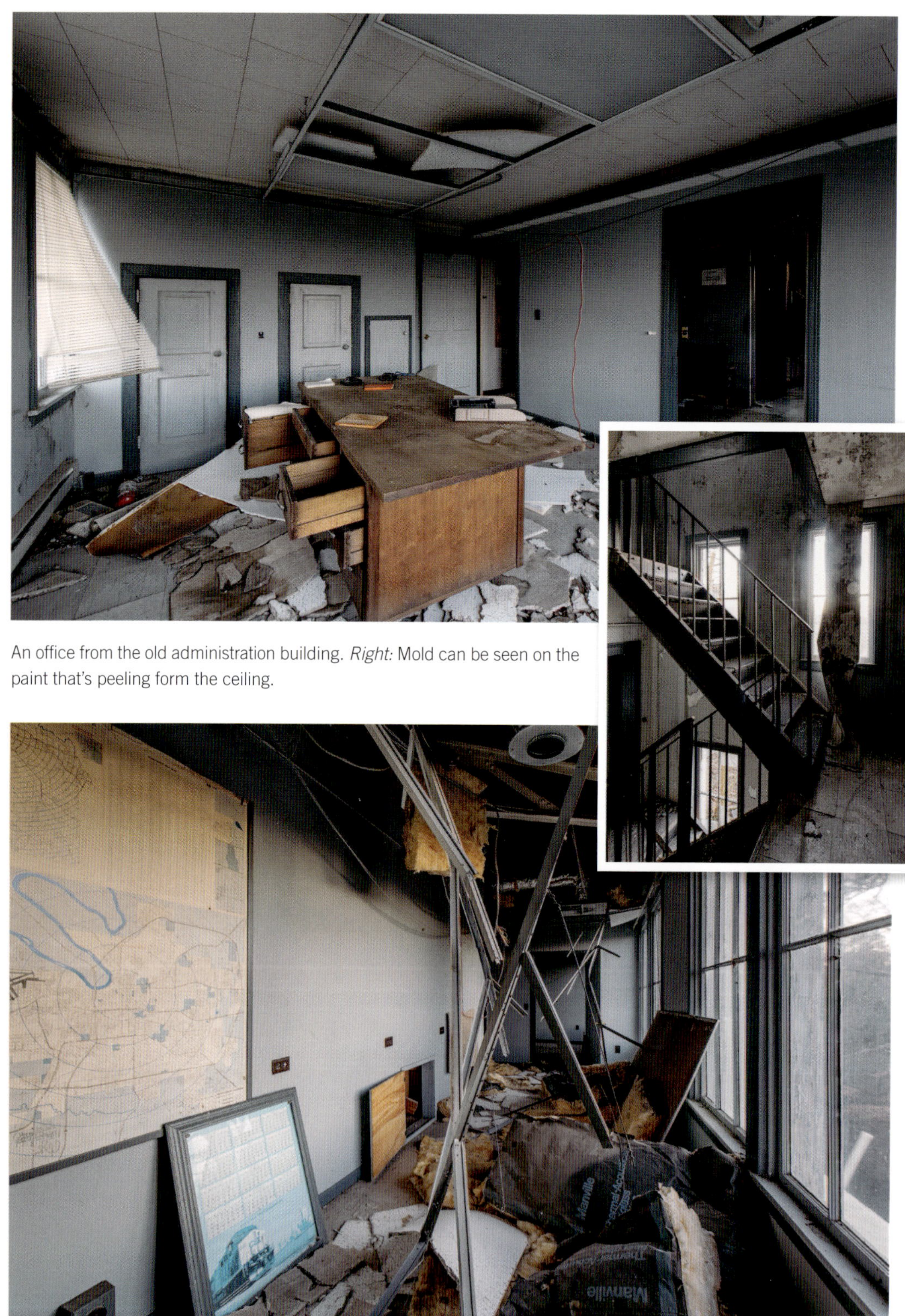

An office from the old administration building. *Right:* Mold can be seen on the paint that's peeling form the ceiling.

A calendar sits on the ground for the year 2000.

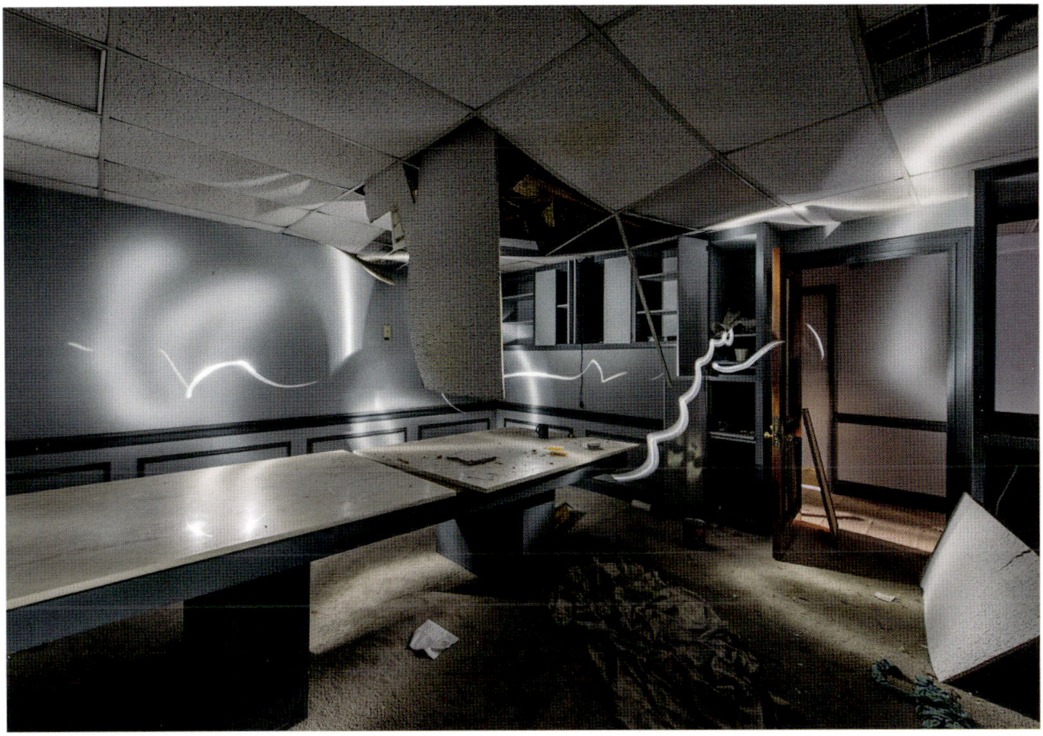

Flashlights illuminate a dark meeting room on the second floor of the building.

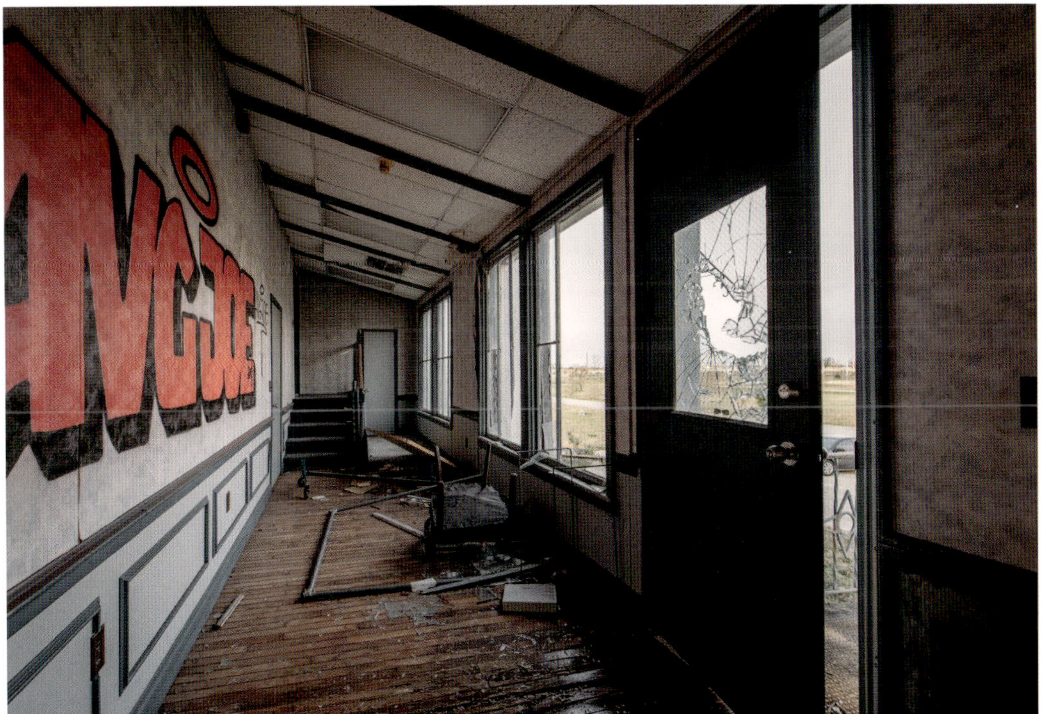

A view of the front entrance.

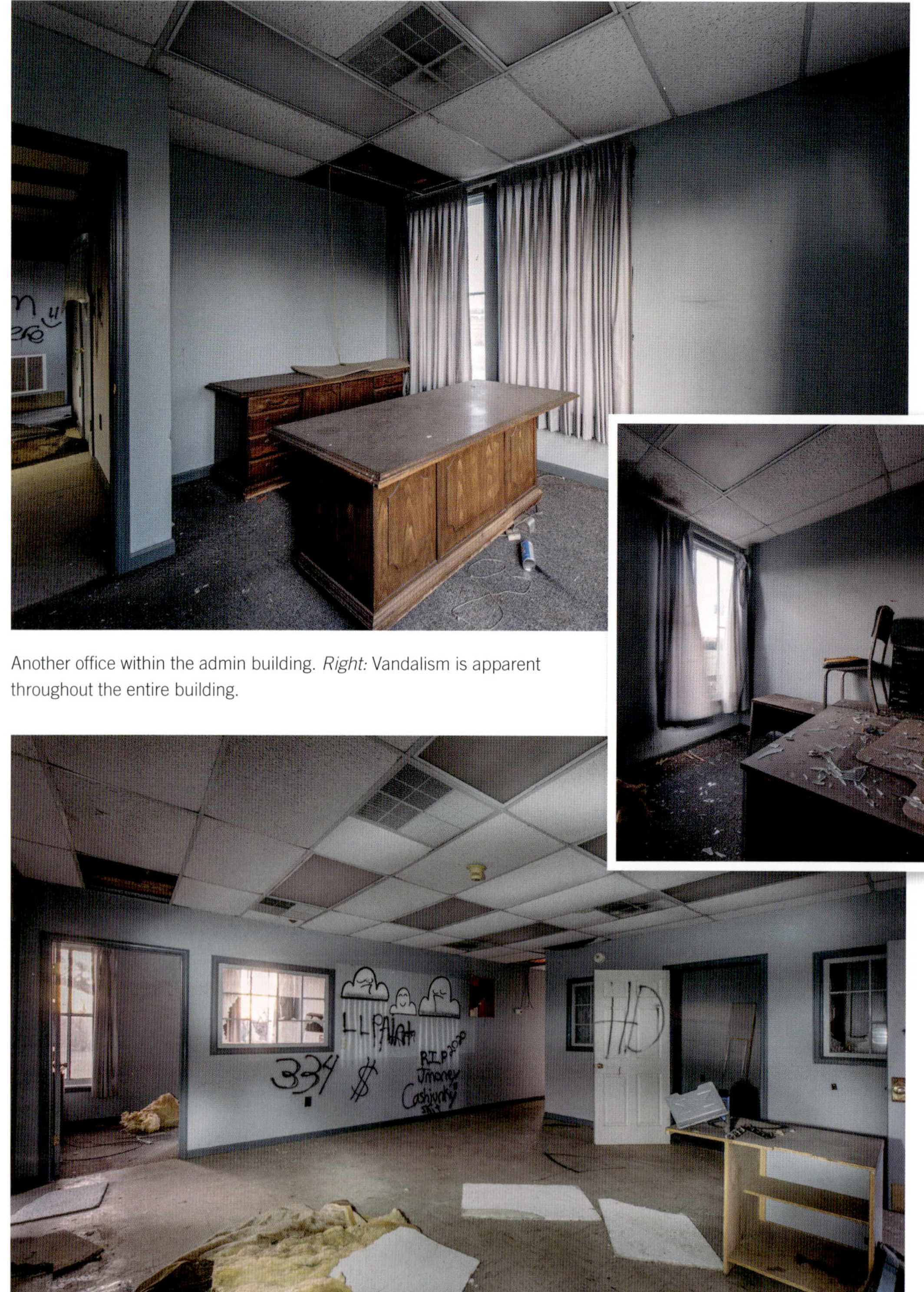

Another office within the admin building. *Right:* Vandalism is apparent throughout the entire building.

The rain cloud graffiti found at the Grove Court Apartments can be found here as well.

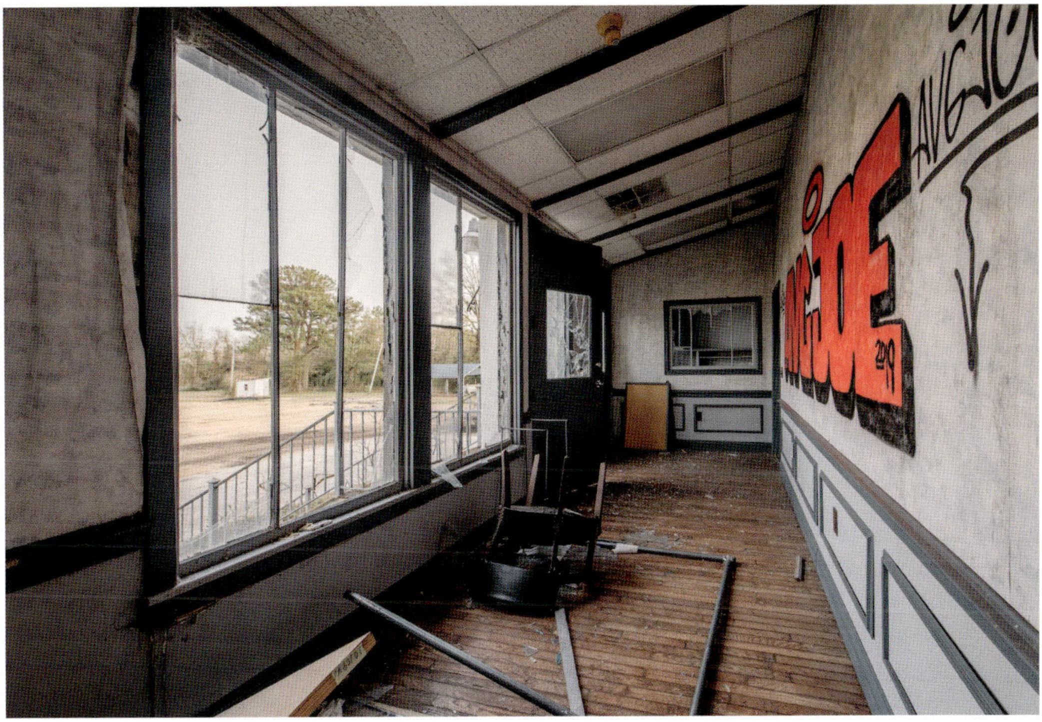

Another view of the front entrance.

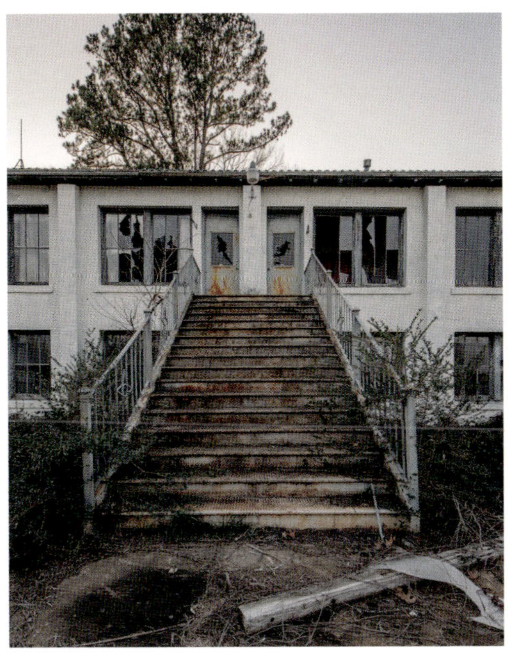

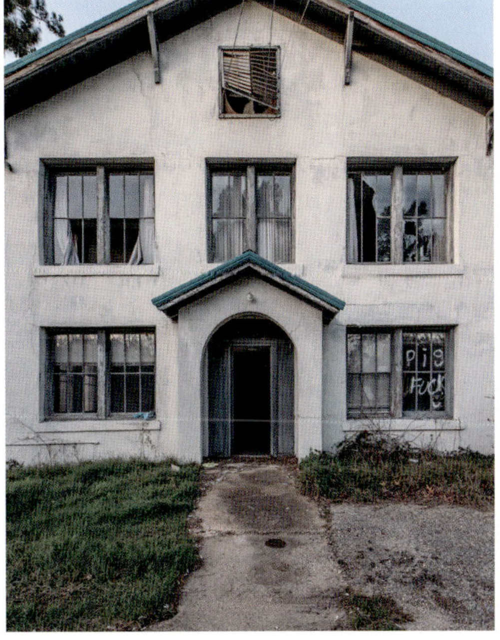

Above left: Looking at the front entrance to the administration building.

Above right: One of many side entrances.

13

THE TOWN OF SPECTRE

Spectre is a fictional town in the 2003 Tim Burton film, *Big Fish*. In the movie, Edward Bloom takes an abandoned path through a haunted forest where he eventually comes upon a small town. The town has no roads lead or cut through Spectre. It contains rows of homes and businesses which lead up to a white church down the middle of them. Built specifically for the film, the movie set is still standing, situated on a small island not far from Montgomery, Alabama.

Though it is private property, the owners allow people to visit the island and even camp there as long as a small payment is made at the gate. Over the years, many of the buildings have either collapsed due to neglect or have been destroyed by fire. The buildings that remain are mostly just facades that are either completely empty or used to house goats.

This shouldn't be said, but if you decide to visit, please respect the animals, campers, and those living nearby. Admission is $3 per person and $10 for overnight camping.

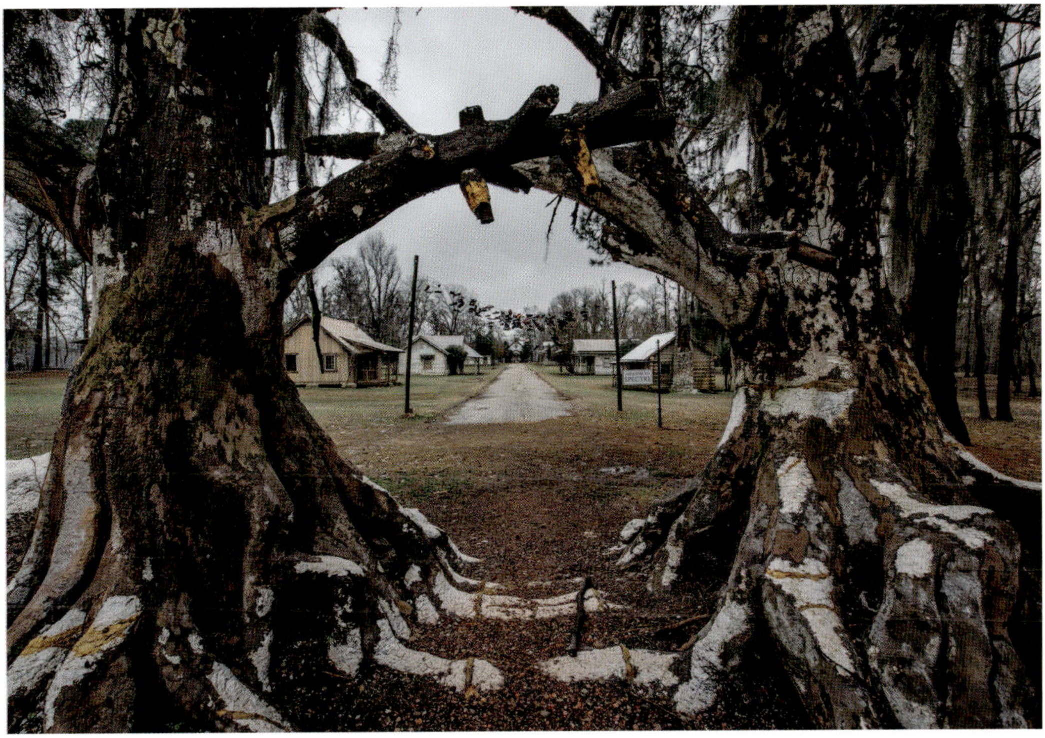

In the movie *Big Fish*, Edward Bloom walks through this pair of trees to enter the town of Spectre.

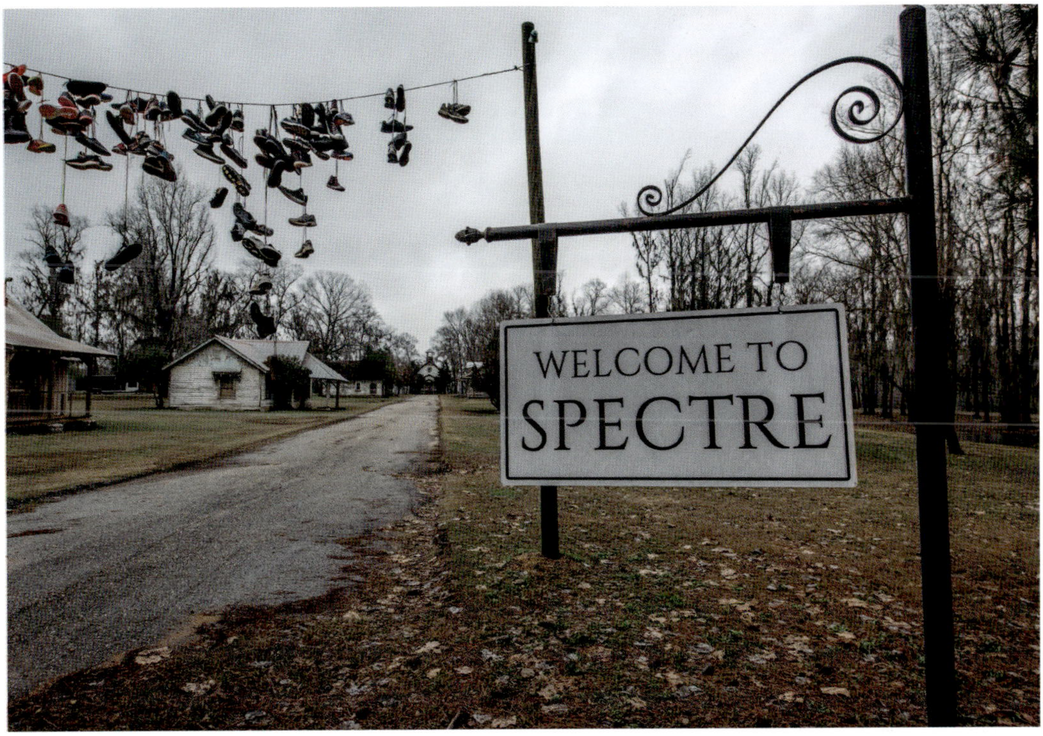

A sign reads "Welcome to Spectre," while shoes thrown by visitors hang on a cable.

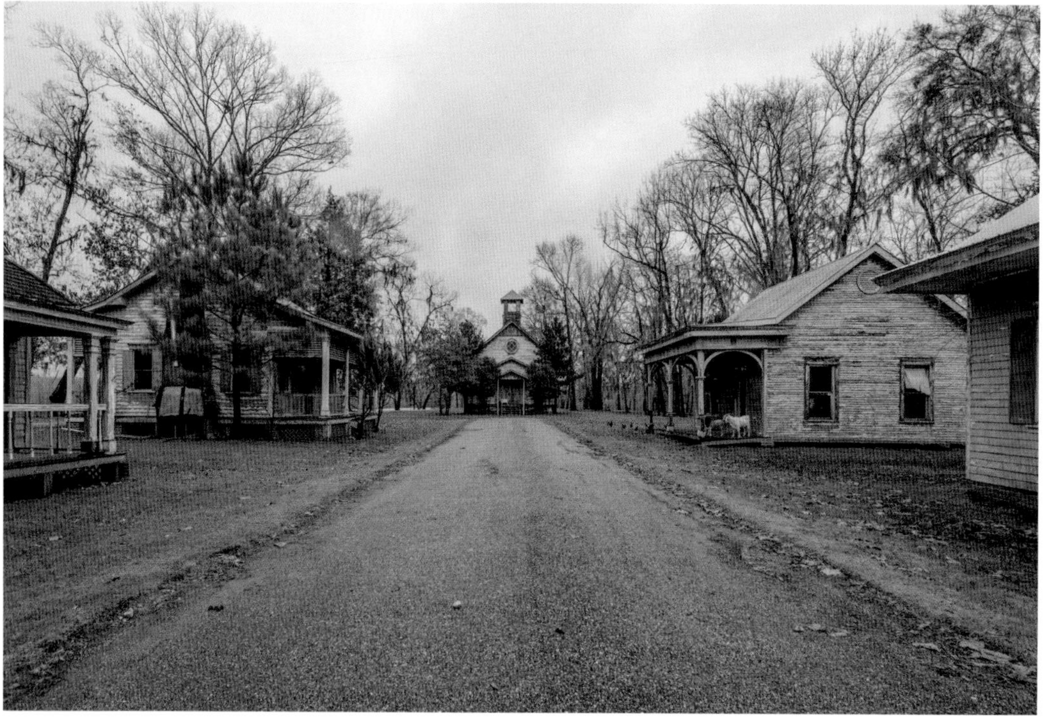

All the buildings here are just shells with no interior built for the movie.

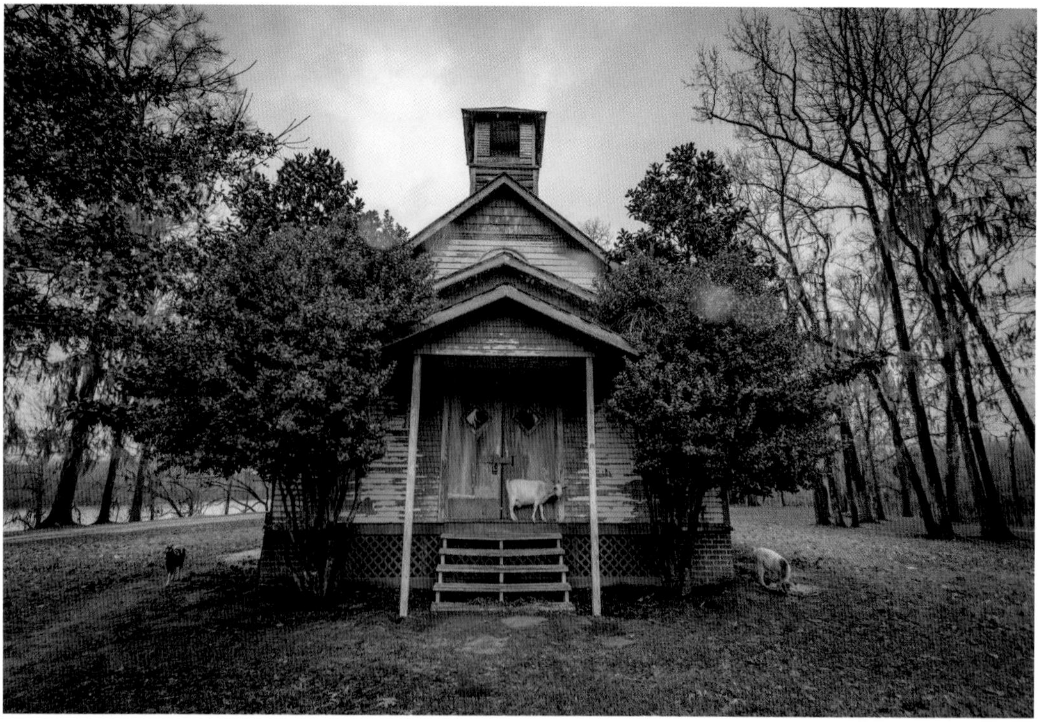

A goat stands against the top of the stairs to the church.

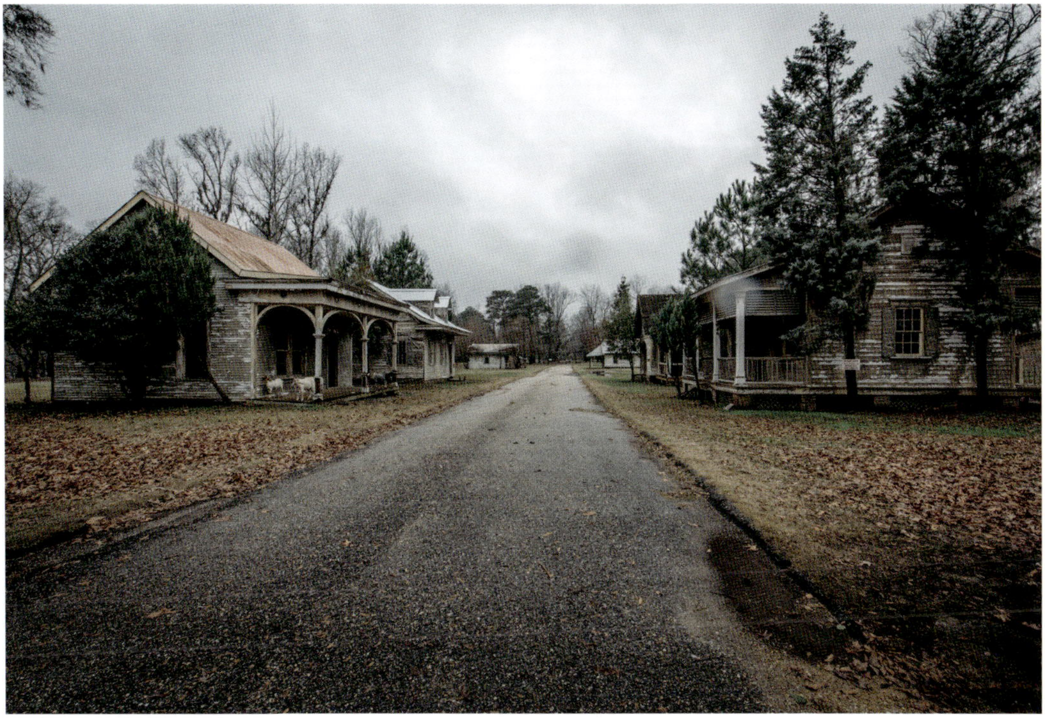

There was once many other buildings as part of the old film set; they have since collapsed due to neglect or destroyed by fire.

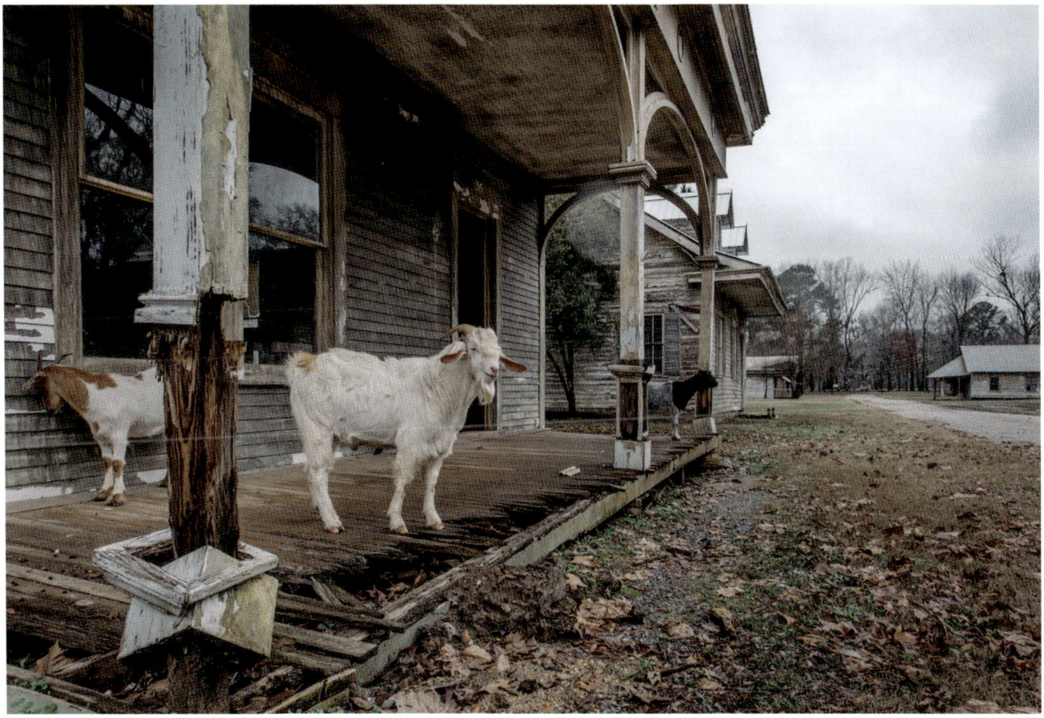

Goats are a common site on the property.

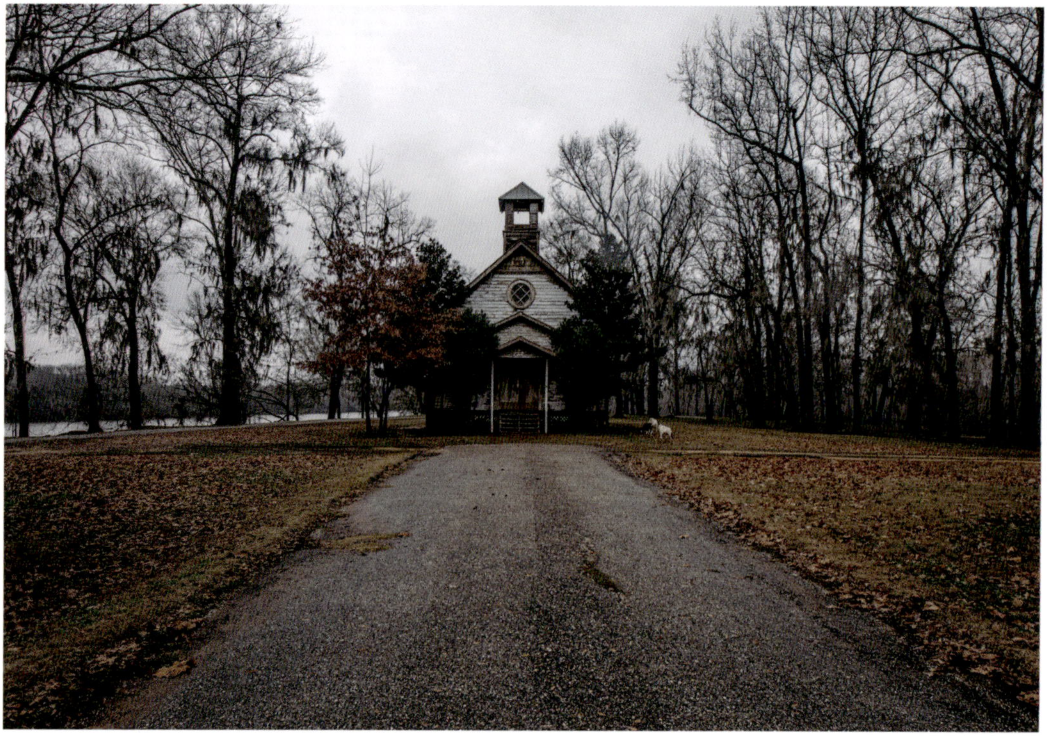

Another look at the church which stands in the center of town.

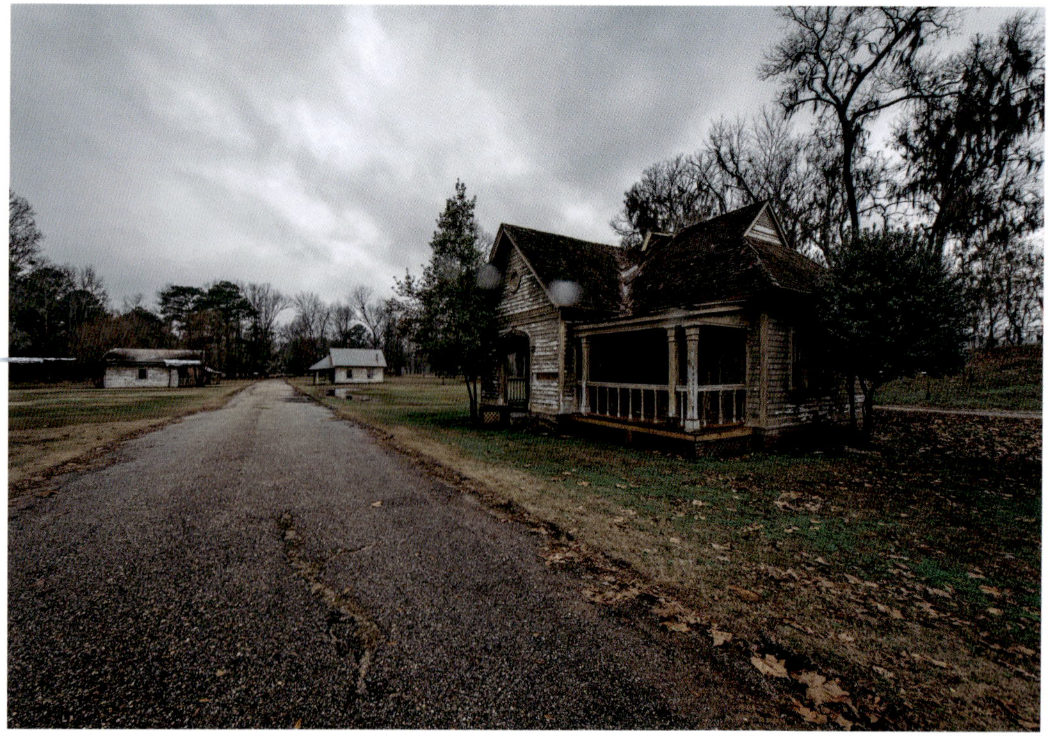

This structure was used as the mayor's house in the movie *Big Fish*.